Linking Language

Linking Language

Simple Language and Literacy Activities Throughout the Curriculum

Robert Rockwell, Debra Reichert Hoge, and Bill Searcy
Illustrations by K. Whelan Dery

gryphon house
Beltsville, Maryland

Text Illustrations: K. Whelan Dery

Library of Congress Cataloging-in-Publication Data

Rockwell, Robert E.
    Linking language : simple language and literacy activities
throughout the curriculum / Robert Rockwell, Debra Hoge, and Bill
Searcy.
        p.   cm.
    Includes bibliographical references and index.
    ISBN 0-87659-202-7
    1. Children–Language. 2. Early childhood education–Activity
programs. I. Hoge, Debra, 1953- . II. Searcy, Leroy, 1953- .
III. Title.
    LB1139.L3R583   1999
    372.6'044—dc21   99-28325
                                                                CIP

Table of Contents

Introduction

What Is Language Development?

To talk about language development, we must first consider the entire concept of *communication*. Communication involves the transmission of a message from a sender to a receiver. This message can be sent verbally (through speech) or nonverbally (through facial expression, body gesture, eye contact, etc.). The written word is also a form of communication, and offers another way to transmit a message. Written language is covered more thoroughly in *What Is Early Literacy* in this introduction.

A message that is sent must also be received in some manner. The receiver hears the message, sees the message, feels the message, or reads the message and usually formulates some type of feedback so the sender knows the message was received.

Even the youngest children know the impact of communication. The child who does not yet have any true words can tell someone to "Pick me up" with a simple gesture of lifting two arms. The child can also let us know that she does not want the peas being spooned into her mouth by the simple act of turning her head or spitting the peas out. Many experts believe that the capacity to communicate is innate in humans, and that we come into this world "ready to communicate."

The development of speech is a key part of human communication. Speech is quite simply a motor act. We inhale by using muscles, cartilage, and bones. We act on the exhalation of air with muscles and spaces within our heads and necks. The sounds that are produced by the tongue, lips, teeth, gums, and soft palate make up the speech sounds of a language. Children need opportunities to practice using these anatomical structures for the production of speech sounds, and the early childhood classroom is a perfect setting for that practice.

Language is defined as a shared set of symbols, and the rules for combining them. You can think of this definition as having two distinct parts. The rules are easier to comprehend. For example, if you are writing, you might stop and think, "*i* before *e* except after *c*, or when sounded as *a* in neighbor and weight." This is an example of a rule of our language.

We have a lot of rules in the English language and the rules change as children mature. It is quite appropriate for a two-year-old to say, "Me go potty." It is not appropriate for a six-year-old to say this. Normally, these rules do not have to be taught, but are acquired by typically developing children. By the time children turn five years old, they usually have an excellent understanding of the rules of our language.

The other part of the language definition deals with symbols. To be a language user, a child must be a symbol user. In order to be a symbol user, a child must have an understanding of the cognitive concepts of object permanence and causality. Object permanence is the ability to know that something exists even if you can't see it. When children develop this skill, they are then able to know that a word stands for something that may or may not be visible. You can say to an eighteen-month-old, "We're going bye-bye. Where are my keys?" At this age the child should know what keys are, and will probably find them before you do! The word or symbol "keys" stands for a real (meaningful) item for the child.

Causality comes into play when children know that a word stands for something (symbol use) and can use that word to cause something to happen. Using the word "no" when offered those mashed peas at dinner is much more socially acceptable than spitting them out at the person offering them. The vocabulary explosion seen in typical two- and three-year-olds is based on the fact that children learn they can cause things to happen with words and that everything around them has a name.

For young children, language development can be divided into two major realms: receptive language and expressive language. Receptive language refers to all that the child takes in. Expressive language is

what the child puts out there for the rest of us to receive. The activities in this book include questions to assess the children's development of the receptive and expressive language abilities embedded within each activity.

What Is Early Literacy?

Amanda, age three, sat on the floor with a group of friends and read *The Wheels on the Bus* to them from memory. Although older than Amanda, the friends listened intently, and none questioned her ability to read the story. Another time Amanda wrote "PBOMMDAMOB" and told her father that it said, "Bring the tape recorder home." When looking at the note later in his office, he put the tape recorder in his briefcase and took it home to her. These are examples of early literacy behavior.

Basic understandings about reading and writing, like oral language, begin long before children reach the traditional school age of five or six. According to a position statement on developmentally appropriate literacy practices published jointly by the International Reading Association (IRA) and the National Association for the Education of Young Children (NAEYC), "Failing to give children literacy experiences until they are school-age can severely limit the reading and writing levels they ultimately attain" (1998, p.197).

As Amanda's behaviors show, the reading and writing skills of young children are quite different from those of adults. For young children to develop literacy skills, they need many opportunities to participate in meaningful activities with print, both through reading and writing, and they need to interact with others who can respond to their reading and writing efforts.

Reading aloud to children from good literature is one of the most important ways to help children develop reading and other literacy skills. Reading aloud, however, means going beyond just reading the words. It involves asking questions, talking about the story and illustrations, and reading the same story a number of times. "It is the talk that surrounds the storybook reading that gives it power,

helping children to bridge what is in the story and their own lives" (IRA & NAEYC, 1998, p. 199).

Young children also need time to explore books on their own. One of the key areas of an early childhood classroom is the library or book center. This center should be well-stocked with a wide range of books, both familiar and new. Children should be encouraged to browse through the books and look at the illustrations or even read from memory, if the books are familiar.

Labels, charts, and signs around the room and the school provide more exposure to print. Children can practice reading signs that label the various centers, as well as instructional signs such as "Knock on the door before coming in." They may return to chart stories that record the details of a field trip to the orchard. By reading the print around their environments, they learn that writing serves a variety of functions: it informs, it entertains, it directs, and it serves as a means for recording ideas for later use.

If children are read to, allowed to explore books on their own, and encouraged to interact with print in their environments, they will develop an understanding of how written language works; that is, they will develop concepts about print. They will begin to learn that print carries meaning and that, in English, reading is from left to right, top to bottom. Young children learn a working knowledge about the alphabetic system of written language. For example, they begin to learn that writing is made up of letters and those letters represent the sounds of spoken language.

These concepts are further supported when children are allowed to express themselves on paper. Early writing for children may involve dictating their words to an adult who writes them down. Young children may express their ideas through drawing. Eventually they will attempt to write using letters and letter-like shapes. It is important for young children to be able to explore writing in these ways. "Classrooms that provide children with regular opportunities to express themselves on paper, without feeling too constrained for correct spelling and proper handwriting, also help children understand that writing has real purpose" (IRA & NAEYC, 1998, p. 202).

A writing center in the early childhood classroom provides opportunities for children to write in a variety of ways. A well-stocked center will include different kinds and sizes of paper; a variety of writing utensils such as pencils, markers, and crayons; small blank books; and items to use when making books, including construction paper for covers, staples, and tape.

Offering literacy materials in other centers of the classroom encourages children to read and write for real purposes. Block builders can write signs telling other children "Do Not Touch." Orders and receipts can be written in the dramatic play area restaurant. Children can record their observations of class pets in special logs or on sheets attached to clipboards. Meaningful writing experiences like these, along with with conversations with peers and adults, provide children with a new understanding of written language and its varied forms and functions.

For literacy skills to develop, young children need many active interactions with print before reaching school age. They need wide exposure to print through reading and writing. Experiences that provide that exposure should be developmentally appropriate. According to the IRA/NAEYC joint position statement, that means literacy experiences for young children should be challenging, but achievable with appropriate adult support. By modeling, encouraging, and supporting literacy experiences in early childhood classrooms, teachers can provide learning experiences that help children begin their journeys as readers and writers.

How to Use This Book

The chapters are organized by areas that are common in most early childhood environments. The activities in each chapter are designed to *initiate* opportunities for children to explore and communicate in active, playful ways as they develop and acquire language and literacy skills.
Each activity contains the following:
● Short introduction—describes the activity and suggests a learning objective
● What to do—simple directions for the activity

● More—suggestions for building on or extending the initial activity
● What you will need—list of materials needed for the activity
● Words you can use—list of words that might be used while the children are engaged in this activity
● Questions—to help you assess the children's emerging language and literacy skill
● Literacy connections/reading experiences—an annotated list of books related to the activity and literacy ideas
● Literacy connections/writing experiences—ways to encourage children to express themselves through drawing, writing, or dictating their thoughts

Using Centers to Support Emerging Language and Literacy Skills

The typical early childhood environment is arranged into areas or centers. These areas commonly include:
● art area
● writing area
● book/quiet area
● block/construction area
● water or sand area
● dramatic play area
● discovery science/math area
● open area for movement activities (indoor or outdoor)

In these interest areas, children are able to explore language and literacy development in active, playful ways as they do the following:
● practice effective expression of needs, wishes, and ideas;
● increase their vocabulary in relevant experiences;
● use language to describe, compare, and relate experiences, thoughts, and feelings;
● create stories, dramas, and songs;
● use language to resolve conflicts;

● use language as a means of securing information;

● are introduced to symbolic representations of language through books, labeling, dramatic play, art, and music; and

● learn about the usefulness of language and writing by activities that link writing to daily experiences;

Early childhood experts agree that learning occurs "primarily through projects, learning centers and playful activities that reflect current interest of children" (Bredekamp, 1987; Katz and Chard, 1989).

It goes without question that centers provide a rich and abundant source of language and literacy development opportunities. All of the center activities presented in this book include language and literacy ideas and activities that give children an opportunity to playfully practice developmentally appropriate oral language and reading and writing in purposeful settings without pressure or expectations.

Family Involvement in Literacy and Language Learning

Children's first teachers are their parents, and therefore their first exposure to language learning and literacy will occur in the home. Parents who talk to and read with their children are providing them with crucial language and literacy activities. As children develop and begin to attend a center or school, the importance of this early learning becomes apparent. When there is frequent communication between home and the center or school, parents can support and continue the language and literacy activities (and any other learning) happening outside the home.

On the next page you will find a form for reporting pertinent information about the day's language development/literacy activity. This form is left relatively open so that it is useable with all activities in this book. Feel free to photocopy this page as needed and use it to share information with involved parents.

References

Bredekamp, S., and C. Kopple, editors. 1997 (revised edition). *Developmentally Appropriate Practice in Early Childhood Programs.* Washington DC: National Association for the Education of Young Children, p. 99.

International Reading Association and National Association for the Education of Young Children. 1998. Learning to read and write: Developmentally appropriate practices for young children. *The Reading Teacher* 52(2): 193-216.

Katz, L., and C. Chard. 1989. *Engaging Children's Minds.* Norwood, NJ: Ablex Publishing Company.

Date:

Dear Parent,

Today our language development/literacy activity was called:

Here is what we did:

Here are some words we used:

The children had fun participating in this activity. Try it at home, if you like.
Your child can help!

Circle Time

CIRCLE TIME AREA

You Are Jumping

With this very simple activity children practice using action verbs in the present tense and the auxiliary verb "are" while engaged in gross motor activities.

What you will need

Picture cards depicting action verbs (made with index cards and markers)

Words you can use

smiling	laughing
jumping	crying
walking	running
skipping	eating
yelling	screaming
tasting	writing
reading	talking
coloring	coughing
climbing	calling
painting	waving
washing	brushing
pushing	pulling
chewing	drinking
dancing	

What to do

● Make picture cards showing verbs that are fun for children to act out.

● Each child takes a turn choosing a card from the pile, and then acting out what the picture shows while the other children guess what the child is doing.

● Encourage the children to use the full sentence, "You are _____."

Questions to assess language development

EXPRESSIVE LANGUAGE

Can the children use the "ing" form of these common action words?

Can the children form the complete sentence "You are _____" with and without a model from the teacher?

Literacy Connections

Two Is For Dancing: A One, Two, Three of Actions by Woodleigh Hubbard

Using bright and wild animal illustrations, this book goes from "1 is for dreaming," to "12 is for balancing."

No Jumping on the Bed by Tedd Arnold

A humorous tale about the perils of jumping on the bed.

Silly Sally by Audrey Wood

First Silly Sally went to town, walking backwards, upside down. But that's not all she did!

WRITING EXPERIENCES

● Take Polaroid photos of individual children in action, then ask the children to write or dictate a page for a class book. Encourage them to write about what they or one of the other children are doing in the photo. For example, "Juan is dancing." Staple the pages together and read the book to the children. Place the finished book in the class library.

● Invite children to keep observations in a learning log. While they observe class pets or animals outside, they can dictate, write about, or draw a picture about what they see, such as "The fish are eating."

Secret Message

The ability to pass a message involves many language and cognitive skills, including auditory memory, listening, and verbal repetition. Here's an activity to pass a simple message and see what comes out at the end!

What you will need

Children in a circle, possibly on
   carpet squares

Words you can use

secret

different

message

turn

listen

same

repeat

What to do

- The children sit in a circle.
- Tell them that the group is going to pass a "secret message" around the circle by whispering it in the ear of the person they are seated next to. The last person will say the message out loud, and then you will state the original message, which may be quite different.
- Tell a "secret message" to the child next to you. The original message should be only two to three words. A familiar message would be good to start with, such as, "Hello, How are you?" or "Happy Halloween."
- Children will listen to see whether the original message is the same or different from the ending message. This activity often has hilarious results!

More

Start the message at different spots in the circle.

Ask a child to start a message.

Literacy Connections

READING EXPERIENCES

Humbug Potion: An A B Cipher by Lorna Balian

An ugly witch finds a recipe for a beauty potion written in a secret code. The translation for the code is written on the book's endpapers.

A Kiss for Little Bear by Else H. Minarik

In this hilarious story, Little Bear's Grandmother gives hen a kiss to take to Little Bear, but before it reaches him the kiss gets passed from animal to animal, and even sets off a little romance between two raccoons.

The Secret Birthday Message by Eric Carle

Tim must follow the secret message written in rebus clues to find his birthday present—a new puppy. The colorful illustrations include cutouts that correspond to the shape clues.

WRITING EXPERIENCES

- Encourage children to write "secret messages" to each other, using whatever kind of writing they want. Then let them read their messages to the receiver.

- Invite children to write a cumulative message to a classmate. One child writes or dictates a sentence, then hands it to the next child. That child adds a message and passes it to the next child, until everyone has added her message. The finished product is then given to the receiver to read. This can be done for a child who is absent, or each child can get a turn being the receiver of the message.

- Invite children to dictate a list of things to do to listen well. Post the list and refer to it regularly to help the children focus attention on their listening.

- If you write a morning message or some other message that you read to the children each day, leave some of the letter out. For example, write "Goo_ mor_ing. To_ay is Mon_ay." Read the message as usual and ask the children if they can tell what is missing. If the children have developed some of the words as sight words, point out that they can still read the word, even if some letters are missing. This is called a "minimal clues" strategy, and points out to readers that it isn't necessary to sound out each letter when we read.

- Plan a treasure hunt in which you place "secret messages" around the room for children to read and follow. Each message should give directions to find the next message until the final message, which leads to the treasure. Use words and/or pictures depending on the ages and abilities of the children.

Questions to assess language development

EXPRESSIVE LANGUAGE

Can children pass on some semblance of the received message to the next person?

RECEPTIVE LANGUAGE

Can children listen and process the message (or some version of the message) as it comes to them?

Stuffed Animal Mystery

This activity demonstrates the powerful use of barriers to promote language, as visual clues are eliminated. One child must describe a mystery item to another child who cannot see it. The child who is guessing will need to pose questions to get more information about the mystery item.

What you will need

Stuffed animals (children could bring from home)

Pillowcase

Box (large enough to cover mystery items)

Words you can use

mystery

sack

guess

clue

think

soft

big

little

small

large

What to do

- One child fills a pillowcase with familiar stuffed animals.
- She tells the other children to close their eyes or to face in the opposite direction.
- She takes an animal from the pillowcase and hides it from view under a box.
- She tells the other children to open their eyes or to turn around.
- She uses words to describe the mystery animal without naming it.
- The other children listen and as descriptions are given, they ask questions that will help them identify the stuffed animal.
- After the stuffed animal is identified, another child takes a turn selecting an animal and describing it to the other children.

More

Describe vegetables that will be eaten at snack.

Describe dolls, toys, objects, or equipment in the classroom.

Questions to assess language development

EXPRESSIVE LANGUAGE

Can children give enough information to allow a reasonable guess?

RECEPTIVE LANGUAGE

Do children listen for descriptive words that enhance their guessing?

Literacy Connections

READING EXPERIENCES

Golden Bear by Ruth Young

> Children will enjoy this rhythmic story about a little boy and his perfect companion, a golden bear.

Jamaica's Find by Juanita Havill

> Jamaica finds a cuddly toy dog in the park and she takes it home. Later, Jamaica finds the girl who belongs to the dog and makes a new friend.

Just Look by Tana Hoban

> Peep through the hole and try to guess what object is in the brilliant photos. Then turn the page to see if you're right.

Where's My Teddy? by Jez Alborough

> When Eddie loses his teddy bear and tries to find it in the woods, he meets a very large bear with the same problem.

WRITING EXPERIENCES

- Make a class chart of the children's stuffed animals. Let children dictate a sentence about their stuffed animal. Record their words on the chart (for example, "Tim brought a yellow dog," or "Miranda brought a shiny, green snake"). Read the chart together, pointing to the words as you read. Leave it up for several days to read again and again.

- Have small blank books available for children to create books about their own stuffed animal. Pages can be used to describe their animal. For example, "My teddy bear is brown. My teddy bear is fuzzy." Encourage them to write, or write their words for them in their books.

- Help children make riddle charts. On large paper children can write or dictate a clue describing one of the stuffed animals. On the back they can illustrate and write the answer. Hang up the charts and read them together.

Hot and Cold

This old game that has been used by children for ages is a rich source of language development. It emphasizes associations, directions, and listening skills.

What you will need

Small items that can be easily hidden in the classroom environment

Words you can use

hot
cold
warm
cool
hidden
near
find
look
search
close
far
eyes

What to do

- The teacher explains to the children that they will be finding hidden items, and that they will receive hints. The hint "hot" means they are close to the hidden object, or are moving towards an item. The hint "cold" means they are not close to the item, or that they are moving away from the item. If necessary, demonstrate this idea for the children.

- Ask the children to close their eyes while you hide an object.

- Chose a child to find the object, using the hints you provide.

- The child attempts to find the object, relying on your hints of "hot" or "cold."

- When the object is found, choose another child to find the next hidden object. To involve all the children, have only the "finder" hide her eyes, while the other children watch you hide the item. Then all the children can help provide the hints "hot" or "cold."

- Play continues as all children get a turn to be the "finder."

More

Depending on the children's abilities, vary the difficulty of the hiding places.

Add the terms "warm" and "cool" as hints.

Questions to assess language development

EXPRESSIVE LANGUAGE

Can the children give accurate hints?

RECEPTIVE LANGUAGE

Can the children associate the word "cold" with being away from the item?

Can the children associate the word "hot" with being close to the item?

Literacy Connections

READING EXPERIENCES

Rebecca Rabbit Plays Hide and Seek by Evelien van Dort

Rebecca Rabbit knows all the best hiding places when she plays Hide and Seek with squirrel, mouse, and hedgehog.

Rosie's Walk by Pat Hutchins

Through full-page illustrations and simple text, the reader follows Rosie, a hen, all around the barnyard, followed by a clumsy fox.

What Game Shall We Play by Pat Hutchins

The animals look for Rabbit over, under, around, and finally in the hole so he can help them decide which game to play.

Where's Spot? by Eric Hill

The hunt for Spot the puppy is on. Questions such as "Is he in the closet?" guide the reader to open the flap to find another animal responding, "No." Finally Spot is found safe in his basket.

WRITING EXPERIENCES

● Encourage children to hide an object, then write or dictate clues for others to use to find it. For example, "If you look by the _____ you will be hot. If you look by the _____ you will be cold."

● Using the pattern of *Rosie's Walk,* make a class book that describes where the children looked for hidden objects. For example, "Marc looked under the art table. Tabitha looked around the block center." Read the book together and place it in the library corner for children to read independently.

Dog Show

This activity allows children to use descriptive words in a fun experience using their very own stuffed animals from home.

What you will need

A note sent home to the parents before the dog show date

Masking tape or another way to put the child's name on her stuffed dog

Blue ribbons (use blue construction paper, scissors, and markers)

Words you can use

black	brown
white	yellow
red	small
tiny	large
big	huge
long	short
pointy	floppy
spotted	tri-color
curly	straight
tail	ear
nose	
eyes	
fuzzy	
describe	

What to do

● Send a note home announcing the Dog Show, asking parents to send a stuffed dog (or other stuffed animal) to school with their child on the designated date.

● On the designated date, the children bring their stuffed dogs to circle time.

● Ask each child to tell something specific that she can see about her dog such as color, size, what kind of fur, what kind of ears, and what kind of tail.

● After each child has had a turn, all participants get a blue ribbon (made from blue construction paper) with DOG SHOW and the year written on it. Everyone is a winner!

More

Ask each child to tell the dog's name.

Ask each child to tell how she received her dog, or where the dog came from.

Encourage the children to engage in pretend play with the dogs.

Categorize the dogs into groups with the children such as brown dogs, white dogs, big dogs, and small dogs.

Questions to assess language development

EXPRESSIVE LANGUAGE

Can the children say descriptive words that really reflect an aspect of their dog?

Can the children say descriptive words in a variety of categories, such as color, texture, size of tail or ears?

Literacy Connections

READING EXPERIENCES

Bears in Pairs by Niki Yektai

> Each page illustrates and describes a pair of bears: "Hairy Bear, Scary Bear, Silly Bear, Frilly Bear." All the stuffed bears end up at Mary's tea party.

I Love Guinea Pigs by Dick King-Smith

> This is an affectionate guide filled with interesting facts about guinea pigs.

Pretend You're a Cat by Jean Marzollo

> Lots of action words encourage the listener to purr, stretch, climb, and leap-just like a cat.

WRITING EXPERIENCES

● On a piece of chart paper, keep track of all the blue ribbon winners. Write the child's name and how she described her stuffed dog. For example, "Tommy's dog: short ears. Kara's dog: long, fuzzy tail."

● Have small blank books available for children to illustrate some of the stuffed dogs brought to school that day, or other stuffed animals around the room or at home. Encourage them to write words to describe the animals, or write their words for them in their books.

● Make a class book by writing a descriptive word on each page. Ask the children to illustrate the book with drawings of their stuffed dogs or pictures cut from toy catalogs.

Group Words

As part of this category and vocabulary building activity, children group animals and then label that group of animals. Some group names will be familiar to the children, while others may be very new.

What you will need

Various animal pictures or small toy animals—fish, kittens, puppies, birds of many types, lions, wolves, horses

Printed word cards with each group name, if appropriate

Words you can use

school	litter
flock	group
pack	pride
covey	picture
various animal names	

What to do

- Put pictures of animals or small toy animals into the center of the circle.
- The children cooperate in putting the "groups" of animals together—fish with fish, lions with lions.
- The children provide or learn the group name for the various animal groups. For example, a *school* of fish, *flock* of birds, *litter* of puppies, etc. Depending on the age and abilities of the children, provide word cards to match each name for literacy development.

More

Pick a group of animals and make the animal sounds.

Learn the words for parents and offspring in each animal group.

Incorporate more difficult group words.

Questions to assess language development

Can the children name the group independently?

Can the children name the group with a prompt?

RECEPTIVE LANGUAGE

Can the children sort the animals into groups?

Literacy Connections

READING EXPERIENCES

All About Alligators by Jim Arnosky

> This beautifully illustrated book will teach children how to tell the difference between a crocodile and an alligator.

A Bundle of Beasts by Patricia Cooper

> This book contains funny poems about unusual collective nouns, such as a smack of jelly fish and a murder of crows.

A Cache of Jewels by Ruth Heller

> Using rhyme, the poet introduces the reader to a host of collective nouns. Some examples include a gam of whales, a kindle of kittens, and a drift of swans.

WRITING EXPERIENCES

● Help children make a dictionary of animal groups. Let each child choose her favorite animal or group name. Have them copy or dictate the group name. Then they can illustrate their page to be put into a class book. Put the finished book in the class library.

I Did/What Did You Do?

Four- and five-year-olds often need practice in responding to questions like, "What did you do today?" This activity gives the teacher another avenue to promote children's expressive language, based on the adult model of asking and answering questions. The children get extra practice as they share their creations with the entire class.

What you will need

Drawing paper

Crayons or paints

Pencil

Words you can use

tell

describe

draw

picture

time references

I TOOK A NAP AFTER LUNCH.

I WENT FOR A WALK IN THE MORNING.

What to do

- Model the sentence structure by saying, "I took a walk in the park yesterday. What did you do?"
- After the children answer ask them to draw a picture of what they did.
- Children make a picture of what they did and use inventive spelling or dictate their description of the activity. Write the dictation on the drawing.
- Give the children an opportunity to describe their drawings to the class.
- Display pictures in the room or corridor of the center. Children enjoy seeing their work on display and the opportunity to share their creations with family members at pick-up or drop-off time.

More

Use other situations such as "I went shopping last weekend. What did you do?" or "I read a book before I went to bed last night. What did you do?"

Incorporate other *wh* questions such as *who, where, why, when* according to developmental appropriateness.

Literacy Connections

READING EXPERIENCES

Birthday Presents by Cynthia Rylant

Proud parents tell their daughter what they did each year on her birthday.

Friends at School by Rochelle Bunnett

Using photographs of a real classroom, children tell what they do during one day at school.

From Head to Toe by Eric Carle

Various animals move their bodies in different ways and ask the children, "Can you do it?"

When I Was Little: A Four-Year-Old's Memoir of Her Youth by Jamie Lee Curtis

A four-year-old tells about things she did when she was younger and what she does now that she's four.

WRITING EXPERIENCES

- After reading *From Head to Toe*, let children move like different animals. Then have children tell how they moved and write or dictate this on a large sheet of paper. For example, "Sara clapped like a seal." "Martin stomped like an elephant." Read the chart together. Hang the chart in the reading corner for children to read on their own.

- Have small blank books available with a title such as "Morning, Noon, and Night." Have children illustrate things they did the day before. Write their words for them below their illustrations. Read their books to them, and have them read to their classmates.

- Make a class book with a title such as "What Did You Do on Your Birthday?" Each child can illustrate something she did on her birthday. The teacher can take dictation using the child's words.

- Encourage children to write, draw, or dictate in a journal each day. Help them think of answers to questions such as "What did you do? Who did you play/work with? Where did you have the most fun?"

Questions to assess language development

EXPRESSIVE LANGUAGE

Can children formulate thoughts and express past tense?

Can children respond to the question "What did you do?" verbally?

Can children describe their drawing of "What did you do?"

RECEPTIVE LANGUAGE

Do children listen as the teacher models "I did _____. What did you do?"

He or She?

A pronoun is a word that stands for something else. In order to use pronouns, children must understand what the pronoun refers to. The use of pronouns is a significant milestone for young children to accomplish.

What you will need

pictures of men or boys doing an activity

pictures of women or girls doing an activity

action figures (optional)

Words you can use

he

she

they

girl

boy

woman

man

doing

what

picture

What to do

● Give each child a picture of a male or female doing some type of activity.

● Ask each child, "What do you see happening in your picture?"

● Each child responds by saying what "he" or "she" is doing.

● If a child does not use the pronoun, she can be prompted by asking, "What is he (or she) doing?"

● The children can take turns pretending to do something and the other children can say what "he" or "she" is doing.

More

Substitute action figures or dolls for the pictures as long as they are clearly male or female.

Questions to assess language development

Do the children use the correct pronoun based on gender?

Do the children use the correct pronoun for a single or multiple subject (*he* or *she* or *they*)?

Literacy Connections

READING EXPERIENCES

Max by Rachel Isadora

Max joins his sister's ballet class to improve his baseball skills.

Sunshine by Jan Ormerod

In this wordless picture book, the morning routine of a young girl, including jobs for her, her dad, and her mom, are sequenced in delightful illustrations.

William's Doll by Charlotte Zolotow

All William wants is a doll. Dad, thinking he knows what boys need, gets him a basketball and a train set. It takes Grandma to know what a little boy really needs—a doll.

WRITING EXPERIENCES

- After drawing a picture of someone in their family, the children can dictate stories about the person.

- Encourage the children to write about their observations of class pets. Help them write about what they see the animal doing, or take their dictation. Use words such as *he, she,* and *they*.

What Does **This** Do?

The older children will enjoy expanding their vocabulary by learning the names of less frequently used household items.

What you will need

Household items that are unfamiliar to the children

Box

Words you can use

tweezers	thermometer
shoehorn	screwdriver
egg beater	spaghetti scoop
whisk	meat mallet
hole punch	rubber band
scale	spatula
paper clip	kitchen tongs
doorstop	recipe
paperweight	slotted spoon
letter opener	
stapler	
phonebook	
cookbook	
pliers	
hammer	

What to do

- Bring out a box of about five to eight household items that are less frequently used in everyday living activities.
- Hold them up one at a time and ask the children what the item is used for.
- Encourage the children to tell or act out what the item is used for. Both modes of information (verbal and visual) should be utilized.
- Once the function of an item has been discussed, ask a child to name the item. (Sometimes the name will come naturally following the discussion of function.)
- Accept all imaginative names and functions, then discuss the actual name and function.

More

Expand this activity into a writing activity using chart paper and markers.

Discuss where the item might be found in the home.

Group the items according to their use—items used in the kitchen, items used at a desk, items used to fix things.

Questions to assess language development

Can the children say what an item is used for?

Can the children name the item?

Literacy Connections

READING EXPERIENCES

Bigmama's by Donald Crews

> While the children visit Bigmama and Bigpapa at their house in the country, they explore all the new things on the farm, in the barn, and around the pond.

Eye Spy, A Mysterious Alphabet by Linda Bourke

> This alphabet book uses clever illustrations to show how words have more than one meaning, such as "eye" of an animal and "eye" of a hook.

The Wind Blew by Pat Hutchins

> The wind picks up objects such as the postman's letters, the groom's hat, and the judge's wig and blows them all around.

WRITING EXPERIENCES

- Help children make lists of objects found in each center in the classroom. Post finished lists near the centers as a check during clean-up to make sure everything gets put in its proper place.

- Have pictures of unusual objects available for children to glue onto blank pieces of paper. Help children write or take their dictation as they describe how the object could be used.

- Help children label and describe how objects around the room are used. For example, "Push the doorstop down to keep the door open." "Use the stapler to fasten paper together." Tape labels around the room and refer to them regularly.

How Do You Use It?

At the age of five children are able to define words in terms of their use. This activity stimulates and reinforces this particular area of language development.

What you will need

Photographs or objects to show the children

Words you can use

ride
car
bus
wear
hat
gloves
sit
chair
bench
eat with
fork
knife
sleep
bed
cot
wash
dishes
clothes
clean
dish
house

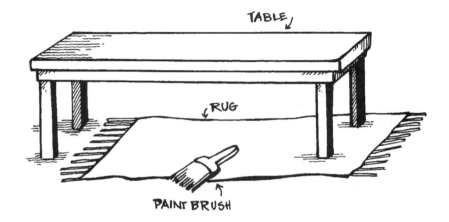

What to do

- Tell the children that you are going to show them some things that we use both at home and here at school. Use photographs or real items if possible.
- Show the children an item. Let the children take turns answering, "How do we use this?"
- Start with items that are available in the center such as a table, chair, rug, block, paintbrush, or paper.
- Now try items of clothing such as shoes, socks, pants, dress, boots, raincoat, or ribbon.
- Now try items that are found in homes such as a bed, sofa, chair, knife, spoon, telephone, or television.

More

Try forms of transportation that are familiar to the children such as planes, car, bus, train, tram, cable car, boat, or ferry.

Categorize the items by use.

Questions to assess language development

Can the children name each item?

Literacy Connections

READING EXPERIENCES

Arthur's Really Helpful Word Book by Marc Brown

Using characters from the popular Arthur books, this book labels objects in a variety of settings, such as school, supermarket, and farm.

Can You Guess? by Margaret Miller

Photographs offer hilarious possibilities and sensible answers to questions such as, "What do you eat for dinner? Blocks? A football? Shoes? Hay? Spaghetti!"

Is It Rough? Is It Smooth? Is It Shiny? by Tana Hoban

Beautiful photographs of the familiar (apples, eggs) and less familiar (bales of hay) lend themselves to many descriptions. The more you look, the more you see.

Snowballs by Lois Ehlert

Each of the snow creatures photographed in this book is finished with a wide variety of real objects. At the end of the book the objects are pictured and labeled.

WRITING EXPERIENCES

- Make a class book by gluing pictures of items on large sheets of paper. Ask the children to describe how they would use each item. Write their words under the picture. After reading the finished book together, place it in the reading center for children to read on their own.

- Encourage each child to make a simple riddle book by folding a piece of paper in half. On the inside glue a picture of a familiar item. On the outside write the child's words as she explains how the item is used. Children can read their books to each other, then place them in the reading center.

- Make word charts similar to *Arthur's Really Helpful Word Book*. Glue pictures from magazines on large sheets of paper. Have the children identify objects in the picture. Write the word on the chart and draw a line from the word to the picture. Then have the children tell how the item is used. Write their words under the label.

Let's Sign

Letting children experience the skill of signing is an enjoyable symbol activity and a new way that children can communicate using simple, everyday signs that are easily readable. This activity can involve those children who are reluctant to speak in a group to participate in a nonverbal manner.

What you will need

Signing reference book such as *The Joy of Signing*

Words (or signs) you can use

any words or signs that are pertinent to the classroom at any given time

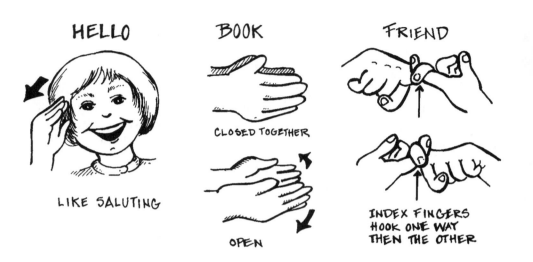

HELLO

LIKE SALUTING

BOOK

CLOSED TOGETHER

OPEN

FRIEND

INDEX FINGERS HOOK ONE WAY THEN THE OTHER

What to do

- The children come to circle time at the beginning of the day.
- The teacher signs "hello" to the group as she also says "hello."
- Each child signs and says "hello" in turn.

More

This activity can be expanded to include the two-word phrase "hello, teacher."

A few signs can enhance any thematic unit.

Questions to assess language development

EXPRESSIVE LANGUAGE

Do the children get the idea that they can say something with their hands?

RECEPTIVE LANGUAGE

Are children curious enough to want to learn more signs?

Literacy Connections

READING EXPERIENCES

Communication by Aliki

This book shows clearly all the different ways we communicate with each other, including braille and sign language.

Handmade Alphabet by Laura Rankin

On each page of this beautifully illustrated book is a hand showing a letter in finger spelling. Along with the hand is an object whose name starts with the letter represented. For example, bubbles float around the sign for B; the hand signing G is gloved.

Handsigns, a Sign Language Alphabet by Kathleen Fain

Each letter of the alphabet is illustrated with a picture of an animal whose name begins with that letter. In the corner of each page is also a drawing of a hand showing the finger spelling sign for the letter.

Handtalk Zoo by George Ancona and Mary B. Miller

This story told with photos, text, and American Sign Language shows a group of children spending the day at the zoo. The adventure is told in both signing and finger spelling.

Joy of Signing by Lottie L. Riekehof

An excellent reference book on sign language.

WRITING EXPERIENCES

● Help children make their own alphabet book of hand signs. Use photos of hands making signs for each of the letters. Glue photos on blank pages. Encourage children to draw, write, or dictate appropriate words on each page.

● Children can write or dictate letters home to families telling about new signs they have learned. Encourage children to take these letters home and to use the new signs.

Healthy Food and Snacks

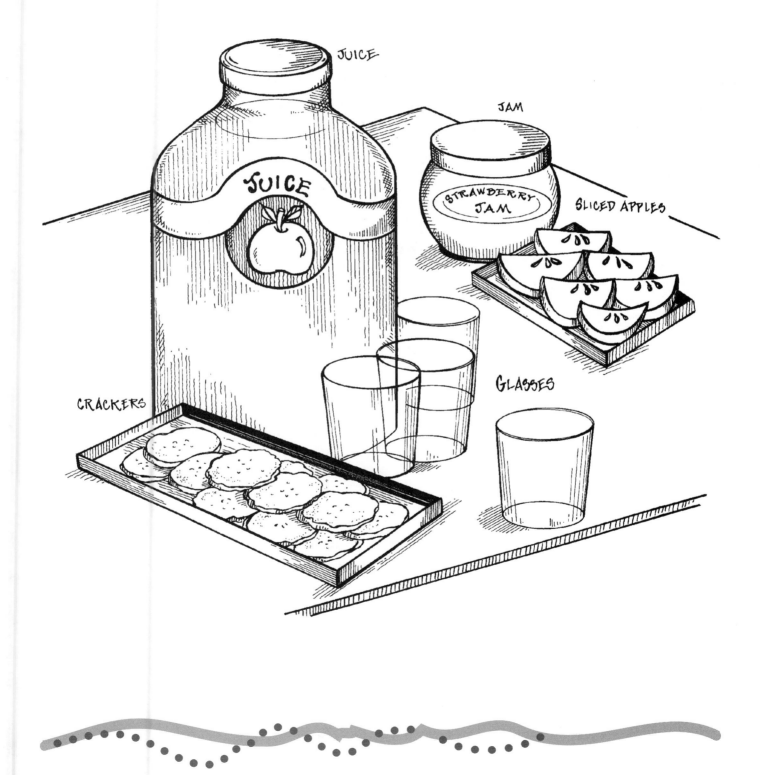

JUICE

JAM

JUICE

STRAWBERRY JAM

SLICED APPLES

CRACKERS

GLASSES

Snack Time

Snack time is a time for teaching children about new foods, for engaging in conversation, and for learning simple etiquette (taking turns and good manners) while children serve themselves, eat, and clean up.

What you will need

Snack foods, such as milk, juice, fruit, crackers

Serving trays

Paper cups

Sponges or paper towels

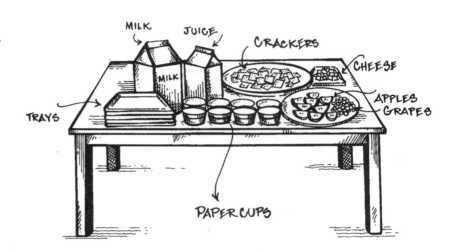

Words you can use

snack

food

please

thank you

time

clean

sponges

paper towels

wipe

wash

manners

spills

accident

talk

listen

quiet

noise

eat

pass

What to do

● Have one or two children serve the snack food, or put the snack on a serving plate and let all of the children pass the food to each other. It's a great time to observe the social rule "take some and leave some."

● Model good manners, encouraging the children to say "thank you" as they receive their snack and "please" when requesting more food.

● Ask the children about other times when they might use the words "please" and "thank you."

● Discuss how we feel when others thank us for something we have done.

● Talk about using the names of classmates to get their attention when they need to pass an item. This is a good way to practice asking for attention in an appropriate manner.

● Have plenty of sponges and paper towels for cleaning up during or after snack.

Questions to assess language development

EXPRESSIVE LANGUAGE

Can children produce politeness markers (please, thank you, etc.) as they engage in passing and receiving food?

RECEPTIVE LANGUAGE

Do children respond to their names as they are passed food items?

Do children respond to good manners as they engage in passing and receiving food?

Literacy Connections

READING EXPERIENCES

Big Black Bear by Wong Herbert Yee

A bear's mother has to teach him manners after he barges into a girl's house without wiping his feet, sneezing without covering his mouth, and threatening to eat her.

Pass the Fritters, Critters by Cheryl Chapman

In this rhyming story, the little boy can't get the animals to pass the food he wants until he begins to say *please* and *thank you*.

Sheep Out to Eat by Nancy Shaw

The sheep in the teashop have horrible manners. Finally, they decide what they really want to eat is the grass outside.

WRITING EXPERIENCES

● Encourage children to write thank you notes to those who provide and prepare snack. Children may draw, write, or dictate their letters.

● Help children keep a snack log. Either on a class chart or in individual logs, children record snacks served each day. They may want to rate each snack as one they liked or disliked.

Setting the Table

The opportunities for communication while preparing the table for snack time are abundant. Setting the table and learning the names of the utensils provide practice in both receptive and expressive language skills. Groups of children using social language while setting the table can increase expressive collaboration.

What you will need

Actual snack food items, magazine pictures of foods, or colored photos (Dairy Council is one source)

Utensils

Place mats with outlines of utensil placement

Words you can use

fingers

hands

knife

fork

spoon

plate

bowl

cup

glass

napkin

set

prepare

table

snack

food

place mat

names of snack food items

What to do

● Ask the children what they use to eat food at home. The responses will probably include the use of their fingers and hands as well as knives, forks, spoons, plates, bowls, cups, and glasses.

● Tell the children that each day when they have snack time, someone will be chosen to set the table for the entire class. Depending on the snack that is served, one or more of the utensils that they mentioned will be used.

● Show the children some snack food items such as apples, grapes, celery, peanut butter, bread, cereal, crackers, milk, juice, or water. As you show each food item, ask the children to name the utensils they would use to eat the sample item. Although finger foods are a common snack, some utensils can be used to eat them or serve them.

● If the snack requires utensils, the children can practice setting the table for this snack. Talk about each commonly used food utensil and how it helps us to eat our food.

More

Ask the children about the snacks they eat at home, and when and how often they eat them. This can be a useful way to talk about nutrition and healthy snacks.

Questions to assess language development

Can children name the utensils and items used in eating?

Can children name a variety of foods?

RECEPTIVE LANGUAGE

Can children identify the various utensils and items used in eating?

Literacy Connections

READING EXPERIENCES

Do Not Feed the Table by Dee Lillegard

This is a book of short poems about kitchen utensils and equipment.

How My Parents Learned to Eat by Ina R. Friedman

Told by a little girl whose mother is Japanese and whose father is American, this book does a wonderful job of presenting different customs within a family, especially the use of chopsticks and knife and fork at the dinner table.

WRITING EXPERIENCES

- Help children make a chart of whose turn it is to set the table for snack. Use a list, a calendar, or another form appropriate for the classroom.

- Invite children to draw, write, or dictate labels for dishes and utensils used at snack and lunch. Tape labels to appropriate cupboards in the kitchen. Make labels for other areas in the classroom.

Yummy Shapes

Cookie cutters come in all sizes and shapes that represent people, objects, and animals. What a great way to elicit both descriptive and expressive language from the children as they create and share stories about the shapes they create and decorate.

What you will need

Fresh bread

Small paintbrushes

Water

Food coloring

Cookie cutters in a variety of shapes and sizes

Chart paper and markers to record the children's dictation

Words you can use

color names

animal names

cookie cutter

cut

shape

design

story

people

occupation names

eat

taste

create

yummy

bread

color

paint

names of shapes

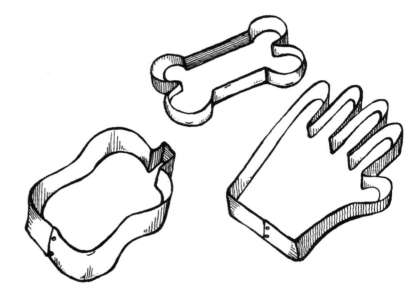

What to do

● Show the children a variety of shapes and sizes of cookie cutters. Talk with them about what they feel the shapes represent.

● Give each child a piece of fresh bread.

● Each child chooses a cookie cutter or cutters from the variety that is provided. If possible, provide cookie cutters in the shapes of people, animals, and objects.

● After cutting out their shapes in the fresh bread, the children paint and decorate them, using brushes to apply a mixture of water and food coloring.

● Encourage the children to use a variety of cookie cutters to create their own unique yummy shapes.

● Ask the children to talk about their creations and the shapes that they represent.

● The Yummy Shapes can be taken home or eaten at snack time.

More

Encourage the children to tell a story about their Yummy Shapes. This can be a collaborative effort with the entire group if desired. These stories can be turned into a classroom book.

Questions to assess language development

EXPRESSIVE LANGUAGE

Can children name what the cookie cutter represents?

Can the children provide descriptive words for their creations?

RECEPTIVE LANGUAGE

Can children identify what particular cookie cutters represent?

Literacy Connections

READING EXPERIENCES

Bread and Jam for Frances by Russell Hoban

> Since Frances refuses to try any new foods, her mother gives her bread and jam for every meal.

Bread Bread Bread by Ann Morris

> Using color photos, this book describes breads eaten all over the world.

● Have a variety of spreads available for the children to choose to put on their bread. As children make their choices, point to the words that name the variety of spread. For example, "You chose grape jelly. This is where it says *grape jelly* on the label.'"

WRITING EXPERIENCES

● Have blank books available cut in the same shapes as the cookie cutters used to cut the bread. Children can use the books to write or dictate about their favorite foods, where they like to eat, or other topics of their choice.

● Take the children's dictation as they describe their bread creations. Hang the finished chart up to read and reread.

● Invite children to create food-shape riddles. They can write or dictate shape and color clues on the front of a sheet of paper. On the back they can draw the food answer.

Cooking and Learning

Children learn lots of things when they cook. Two things they might learn are that words have value, and that reading is something that can be personally exciting and useful. They can also learn how to follow a sequence, both verbally and in writing with this No-Bake Cookie Recipe.

What you will need

Recipe poster

Large mixing bowl

Large spoon

Measuring cups

Plastic gloves for each child

½ cup (125 ml) wheat germ

1½ cups (325 ml) peanut butter

1½ cups (325 ml) brown sugar

3 cups (750 ml) dried milk

¾ cup (190 ml) graham cracker crumbs

Powdered sugar

Words you can use

measure	ingredients
cup	count
cookies	spoon
mix	name
tablespoon	teaspoon
picture	paper
recipe	read
food	water
milk	margarine
flour	bowls
sugar	top
bottom	stir
heat	baking powder
paper towels	write

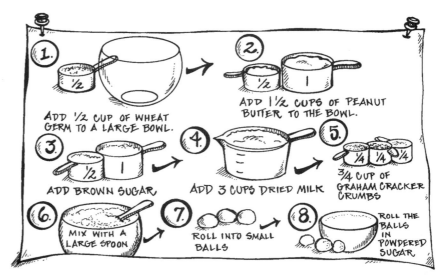

Food, Nutrition and the Young Child, 4th ed., by Jeanette Enders and Robert E. Rockwell, ©1994. Reprinted by permisson of Prentice Hall, Inc., Upper Saddle River, NJ.

Before the activity

Make a large recipe poster that is illustrated so a young child can read it independently. A properly organized recipe gives the child the pre-reading skills of top-to-bottom and left-to-right sequencing. Most recipes as they appear in cookbooks do not do this. Usually the ingredients are listed, followed by a series of instructions. Rewrite the recipe on a large poster so that cooking can progress from the first to the last step in sequence. Save the poster recipes so they can be used again and again. Recipe posters also teach a variety of math concepts such as number recognition, counting, and measurement. An illustrated recipe also gives the children who are waiting their turn something to refer to as they help count the ingredients being added.

What to do

- Label each ingredient and utensil that the children will use.
- Display the recipe poster and read it with the children.
- The children take turns preparing the cookie dough as they follow the picture recipe for No-Bake Cookies (this recipe makes about 50 cookies if the balls aren't too big).

- Measure ingredients into a bowl and mix them with a large spoon or have some fun and let the children use their hands to do the mixing.
- When ingredients are thoroughly mixed, have the children use their fingers to take small amounts of dough from the mixture and roll them into small balls about an inch (3 cm) in diameter.
- The children then roll the balls in powdered sugar and they are ready to eat.

Note: Remember not to belabor each step or insist that the children understand each concept. Treat the recipe as a tool. Ask occasional questions about what they are doing, and let the children's comments and questions guide the discussion.

Questions to assess language development

EXPRESSIVE LANGUAGE

Can children name (label) the tools and ingredients used for the recipe?

RECEPTIVE LANGUAGE

Can children identify the various tools and ingredients used for the recipe?

Can children follow a sequence in making the recipe?

Literacy Connections

READING EXPERIENCES

Benny Bakes a Cake, by Even Rice

Preschoolers will enjoy this story about Benny and his birthday cake. They will especially like Ralph the Dog, who can't resist digging into the fresh-baked cake.

Mr. Cookie Baker, by Monica Wellington

Mr. Cookie Baker mixes, cuts, and bakes delicious cookies for his customers. Includes a recipe for sugar cookies.

WRITING EXPERIENCES

- Record the cooking experience on a piece of chart paper. Take children's dictation. Read the chart to the children and encourage them to read the chart throughout the day.
- Have cookie-shaped books available for children to draw and write in.
- Help children graph the group's favorite cookies. They can write their names under the label for their favorite cookies; they can write their name on a cookie-shaped paper and attach it to the graph; or they can use tally marks to indicate their favorites.

Yummy, Yummy

Children love to talk about eating, especially eating in a restaurant. Children who have not eaten in a restaurant can listen and learn.

What you will need

Simple picture menus with food items for each mealtime cut from food magazines

Pot, pans

Paper plates

Plastic eating utensils

Small notepads, pencils

Cash register and play money (optional)

Small table, tablecloth, table decorations

Words you can use

restaurant	waiter
server	greeter
cashier	order
write	pad
pencil	menu
breakfast	lunch
dinner	meal
table	cook
eat	pay
owe	chair
names of foods	

What to do

● Talk about eating at a restaurant. Ask children if they have eaten at a restaurant and how they liked it.

● Ask them what happened after they entered the restaurant. (They might talk about being seated, looking at a menu, ordering food, eating, paying the bill.)

● Set up a restaurant center. Encourage the children to make picture menus for breakfast, lunch, and dinner meals. If possible, have order books and pencils for the servers; pot, pans, and utensils for the cooks; and cash register and pay money for the cashiers.

● Decorate a table with a tablecloth and flowers. Although any arrangement that arises from the children's experiences can work, the center described here can accommodate eight children: one to four seated at the table, one cash register operator and greeter, one server, one cook, and one dishwasher.

✓ The greeter sits the patrons at the table and passes out the picture menus.

✓ The server takes orders and writes them on the order pad, perhaps using inventive spelling.

✓ The server passes the order to the kitchen where the cook prepares it.

✓ The server takes the completed order to the table where it is eaten.

✓ The server gives check to customer who pays at the cash register.

More

Talk about and set up other types of places where food is ordered and consumed such as a fast-food restaurant or drive-in restaurant.

Make a graph of the children's favorite restaurant foods or restaurants.

Questions to assess language development

EXPRESSIVE LANGUAGE

Can children answer questions about their restaurant experiences?

Can children use appropriate language in the restaurant center?

RECEPTIVE LANGUAGE

Can children identify items connected with the restaurant script?

Literacy Connections

READING EXPERIENCES

Animal Café by John Stadler

When the restaurant closes down at night, Casey the cat and Sedgewick the watchdog open it back up for all the neighborhood animals.

Dinner at the Panda Palace by Stephanie Calmenson

Mr. Panda's restaurant seems to have room for everyone. In this rhyming story, groups of animals from one to ten are accommodated.

In the Diner by Christine Loomis

A typical day in a diner is told in rhyming verse.

WRITING EXPERIENCES

● Enlist the help of the children to make the menus. They can dictate captions for the pictured items. They may also want to draw, write, or dictate their own menus.

● Invite the children to make signs for the restaurant, including the name of the restaurant, open and closed signs, and advertisements.

Mystery Raisins

Talking about foods that are being served for snack or lunch can be a useful tool to encourage children to eat nourishing food.

What you will need

Raisins

An opaque container with holes cut in the lid

Words you can use

raisins	hole
smooth	square
color	smell
rough	squishy
big	taste
wrinkled	color names
large	eat
soft	mystery
little	lunch
hard	guess
small	snack
round	container
tiny	meal
flat	

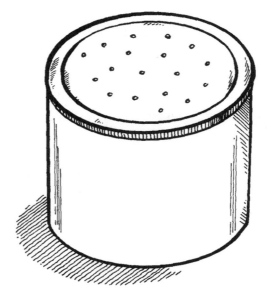

What to do

- Place some raisins in an opaque container with holes in the lid.
- Have each child smell the raisins that have been placed in the container.
- Ask them not to guess what is in the container until everyone has smelled the raisins.
- Now ask those who think they know to raise their hands but not to name the mystery item.
- Next ask the children to close their eyes. Hand each child a few raisins and have them describe the mystery item. They may use the words small, squishy, wrinkly, soft, round, and even square.
- Ask the children to open their eyes to check their identification. Talk about their observations and ask questions such as what color is a raisin? How big is it? Is it smooth? What do you do with it? What does it taste like?

More

Talk about how raisins are dried grapes. Hang a bunch of grapes from the ceiling. Cover the grapes with cheesecloth and set to dry in the sun. Let the children observe the changes in the grapes and try to guess what will happen next.

Try this with other snack or lunch foods.

Questions to assess language development

EXPRESSIVE LANGUAGE

Can children label raisins by name?

Can children use descriptive terms for the raisins?

Literacy Connections

READING EXPERIENCES

Eating the Alphabet: Fruits and Vegetables from A to Z by Lois Ehlert

This beautifully illustrated alphabet book focuses on fruits and vegetables.

Mr. Rabbit and the Lovely Present by Charlotte Zolotow

A little girl tries to find the perfect present for her mother. With the help of a large rabbit she put together a basket of fresh fruits.

What Am I? Looking Through Shapes at Apples and Grapes by N. N. Charles

A rhyming guessing game about fruits, colors, and shapes. Readers read clues, guess the fruit being described, and turn the page to reveal the answer.

WRITING EXPERIENCES

● Include a series of containers holding a variety of foods. Number each container. Invite children to write or draw their predictions of what's in each numbered container.

● Have blank books available for children to create "Good Smell/Bad Smell" books. They can label pages in their books "Smells Good" and "Smells Bad." Then they draw, write, or dictate names of foods that fit in each category.

Food Colors

Fruits and vegetables come in a variety of colors. Develop children's awareness of color and observation skills by looking at pictures of fruits and vegetables or the actual fruits and vegetables that you bring into the classroom. Names (labels) for fruits and vegetables are the language focus here.

What you will need

Newsprint

Masking tape or easel

Crayons

Variety of foods, pictures of foods from magazines, or color photographs of foods

Words you can use

mark

draw

color

like

dislike

taste

count

chart

names of colors

names of foods

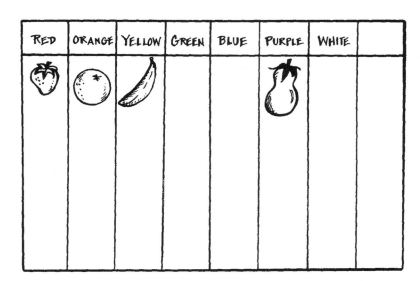

What to do

- Make two color tally charts on large pieces of newsprint (see illustration). Each chart should be divided into eight columns. Each column is for recording one color. Keep one column open for colors that do not match those presented.
- Bring out one fruit or vegetable. After the item is identified, ask the children, "What color is it?"
- After the children respond, let them take turns taping the picture in a column, making a mark in a column, or drawing the item in the matching color column with a crayon of a corresponding color.

More

Count the colors in each column. Which one is used the most often? Which one is used the least often?

Graph the colors of the clothing the children are wearing to school on two separate days.

Graph the children's favorite colors.

Questions to assess language development

EXPRESSIVE LANGUAGE

Can children name various colors seen on the food?

Can children state an opinion whether they "like or dislike" a certain food?

RECEPTIVE LANGUAGE

Can children sort foods by color?

Literacy Connections

READING EXPERIENCES

Cloudy with a Chance of Meatballs by Judi Barrett

> A town is used to edible precipitation. But one day, the weather turns very nasty.

Growing Colors by Bruce McMillan

> This book shows brilliant color photos of fruits and vegetables growing on vines, plants, and trees.

Growing Vegetable Soup by Lois Ehlert

> Brightly-colored illustrations of vegetables and gardening tools are labeled. A simple recipe for making soup is included.

● Bring in empty food cartons and labels to place in the reading center or dramatic play center. Invite children to read and talk about them. Labels and cartons can be sorted by color, kinds of food, etc. Cartons can be props in the dramatic play center.

WRITING EXPERIENCES

● Make a class chart of the children's favorite foods. Separate charts can be made for different food colors, such as "Our Favorite Red Foods" or "Orange Foods We Like."

● As children try different foods, encourage them to keep simple logs of their likes and dislikes. Fold an 8 ½" by 11" (21 cm x 28 cm) piece of paper in half. On one side the children draw, write, or dictate foods they like. On the other, they record the foods they dislike.

Recipes for Our Favorite Foods

All children have favorite food dishes and unique perceptions as to how those dishes are prepared. In this activity, the children share their perceptions of their favorite recipes. This activity can be done individually or with a small group.

Note: Do this activity after the children have an understanding of the meaning of a recipe.

What you will need

Paper and crayons
Stapler and staples

Words you can use

recipe
amounts
stir
mix
how much
food names
ingredients
shake
cook
stove
microwave
pot
cups
spoon
bowl

CHICKEN and RICE

What to do

● Talk about and share the recipe that the children followed when they prepared the No-Bake Cookies (see page 46).

● Remind the children that a recipe tells us how to make something that we want to eat. When meals are prepared at home or in a restaurant, the person who is cooking usually follows a recipe just like the one for No-Bake Cookies.

● Tell the children that you want them to tell you what they think is the recipe for one of their favorite dishes. Ask the children to draw their favorite dish on a piece of paper.

● Once the children have identified the dish, ask them to dictate their interpretation of the recipe as you record ingredients and amounts on paper or a tape recorder.

● Put the accumulated pictures and recipes in a booklet that can be sent home to share with the children's families.

Questions to assess language development

EXPRESSIVE LANGUAGE

Can children tell a sequence using the words *and, then,* or *next*?

Do children use some type of written language component with their recipes?

Can children use specific words as they dictate their own recipes?

Literacy Connections

READING EXPERIENCES

Beware of Boys by Tony Blundell

A little boy who gets captured by a hungry wolf offers the wolf some recipes for Boy Soup, Boy Pie, and Boy Cake. As the wolf searches for the ridiculous ingredients the boy escapes and gets home in time for his own supper.

Everybody Cooks Rice by Nora Dooley

Carrie goes from house to house looking for her brother. At each house she samples different recipes from around the world. Nine recipes for rice dishes are included.

● Place some of these or other appropriate cookbooks in the class library or dramatic play center:

Cooking Art: Easy Edible Art for Young Children by MaryAnn Kohl and Jean Potter

Cup Cooking by Barbara Johnson and Betty Plemons

Fun With Kids in the Kitchen by Judi Roger

Quick and Easy Cookbook by Robyn Supraner

● In the dramatic play center, place food cartons that have directions for preparation printed on them. Children may help prepare some of the different foods, such as instant pudding, while you model reading the directions.

The Food Pyramid

The United States Department of Agriculture developed the Food Guide Pyramid to help consumers plan nutritionally sound diets and to promote good eating habits for both children and adults. Pictures on the pyramid show the food groups. In this activity the children are encouraged to name (label) and categorize various food items, targeting both receptive and expressive language.

Note: This is an advanced activity.

What you will need

Chart showing the USDA Food Guide Pyramid. It can be obtained at no cost from the US Department of Agriculture in Washington, D.C.

Pictures of food (available from the Dairy Council or cut out pictures from food magazines)

Food that is served for breakfast, lunch, or snack

Small paper plates or napkins

Poster board

Markers

Words you can use

food	pyramid
remember	healthy
like	good
bad	favorite
yucky	sick
dislike	eat
think	share
lunch	supper
dinner	breakfast
snack	names of foods
triangle	shape

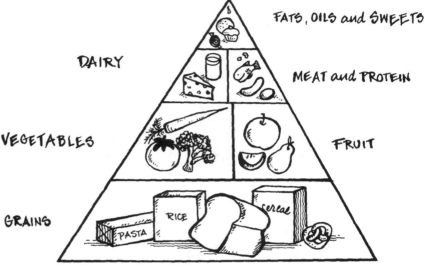

What to do

- Show the children the Food Guide Pyramid. Let them take turns identifying the foods at each level of the pyramid.

  The bread, cereal, rice, and pasta group is at the base of the pyramid. Grain based foods are rich in complex carbohydrates including fiber, vitamins, and minerals and should make up the bulk of the diet with six to eleven servings per day. The phrase "five a day" is used frequently to refer to the five fruits and vegetables that are next on the list of priorities. Depending on your age, two to three servings from the dairy products group as well as the meat or meat alternates group are recommended. Fats, oils, and sweets take up the least space at the pyramid's narrower tip because they should be given the lowest priority in a healthful meal plan.

- Draw a large pyramid on a large piece of poster board. Use a marker to divide the pyramid into six sections (see illustration). Place the finished drawing on the floor.

- Gather the children into a large circle around the pyramid drawing.

- Place a small portion of one food item that they will be eating at lunch or snack on a small paper plate or napkin. Let the children identify and share what they know and feel about their food item. Tell the children that it's okay if they dislike or prefer certain foods. Give them the opportunity to talk about which foods they like and don't like to eat and have them explain why.

- Using the USDA Food Pyramid as a guide let the children place the real food (on the napkin) that they will be having for lunch or snack into the appropriate section of the pyramid.
- Discuss the importance of eating a variety of foods from all the groups and that all the foods that we eat can help us grow.

More

Talk about the foods that the children had for dinner last night. Record the foods on a chart as the children talk. Follow the steps in the original activity. Do the results show that the children are eating balanced diets? This activity presents an excellent opportunity for a newsletter article that can be sent to families about learning the importance of a balanced diet and how the USDA Food Pyramid can help them understand how to eat a balanced diet.

Let the children choose a colored picture of a food item that they would like to be. Then encourage all the children to stand where the foods would be in the Food Pyramid, creating their own living pyramid. If steps are available, this will increase the visual aspect of the pyramid.

Take a photograph of this "living triangle," and send a copy of it home with each child to promote conversation.

Literacy Connections

READING EXPERIENCES

Dinosaurs Alive and Well? A Guide to Good Health by Laurence Krasny Brown

The authors use dinosaurs to explain the basics of nutrition.

Nutrition by Leslie Jean LeMaster

This book covers the basics of nutrition for beginning readers. Includes color photos.

- Read food labels with the children. The labels can be categorized and placed on the food pyramid.
- Bring in menus from restaurants or use the school menu. Invite children to identify the types of foods served.

WRITING EXPERIENCES

- Encourage children to keep logs of the foods they eat. In blank books, have them write or dictate each day the food eaten at meals and snacks. At the end of the week, they can categorize their choices to see how balanced their eating was.
- Invite the children to write menus, either for restaurants or school. Help them plan menus that offer a healthy balance of foods.

Questions to assess language development

EXPRESSIVE LANGUAGE

Can children name a variety of foods?

Can children name foods by category?

RECEPTIVE LANGUAGE

Can children identify foods by names?

Can children identify foods by category according to the food chart?

Supermarket Classification

A field trip to the grocery store or supermarket is an excellent follow-up to The Food Pyramid. The opportunities to use both receptive and expressive language abound in this activity, as does the idea of generalization. Children generalize the knowledge they have from picture cards into actual items.

Note: This is an advanced activity.

What you will need

Copies of the Food Guide Pyramid. Photocopy it from cereal boxes or ask the children's families to collect them from the boxes at home.

Approval for the field trip, permission slips

Notepad and pen or pencil to take notes of the children's comments for later discussion and sharing

Words you can use

food	like
dislike	manager
cash register	money
shop	family
favorite	meat
vegetables	produce
help	cart
basket	park
aisle	shelf
freezer	clerk
food names	checkout clerk
cashier	food groups

food guide pyramid

nonfood items such as magazines, shoe polish, toothpaste, etc.

What to do

● Review the food groups that are detailed in the Food Pyramid. Display the Pyramid and let the children point out, name (label), and describe the food groups.

● After arriving at the store distribute one card to each child that has the Food Guide Pyramid printed on it.

● As the children tour the store and its various sections, let them take turns pointing out food items and telling where the foods fall on the Food Pyramid. For example, in the produce section, the child points to and names a carrot. He then shows the group and tells them that the carrot goes into the fruit and vegetable section of the pyramid.

● Encourage the children to ask questions about foods that are unfamiliar to them. There may be some foods that you will not recognize. This presents an excellent opportunity for the teacher to model questioning language by asking the produce manager about food names as well as geographical origins.

More

As the class tours the store, let the children point out and tell you the names of nonfood items that they see.

Talk about the various sections of the store.

Talk about the children's food likes and dislikes.

Discuss how the children can help their parents when they shop for groceries.

Questions to assess language development

EXPRESSIVE LANGUAGE

Do children name a variety of food items?

Do children name category words for foods?

RECEPTIVE LANGUAGE

Do children identify foods by name?

Do children identify foods by categories?

Literacy Connections

READING EXPERIENCES

At the Supermarket by David Hautzig

  Photographs show items to buy and work that is done at a supermarket.

Just Shopping with Mom by Mercer Mayer

  A simple tale of a shopping trip that includes a grocery store.

The Storekeeper by Tracey Campbell Pearson

  This is a story of a storekeeper and her busy day.

We Keep a Store by Anne Shelby

  A little girl tells all about her family owning and running a store.

● While at the supermarket, read food labels and encourage children to read food labels, too.

● Have food ads from local supermarkets available in the classroom. Children can read through the ads, cut out pictures of various foods, and classify them according to the Food Pyramid.

WRITING EXPERIENCES

● Before the field trip, ask the children, either in a group or individually, to write or dictate letters to their families, requesting permission to go on the field trip.

● While at the supermarket, encourage the children to make observational drawings. Back in the classroom, children can write or dictate captions for their drawings. Hang the finished illustrations in a display. Read the captions and encourage the children to read theirs and other children's captions.

● Encourage children to write thank you letters to the supermarket personnel, transportation providers, and so on.

Dramatic Play

DOLL

DOLL BED

HAT

PLASTIC FOOD

TOY CASH REGISTER

TOY TELEPHONE

PLAY MONEY

BALL HAT

A Shopping We Will Go

Children love to talk about food and pretend to do the jobs of the people in stores.

What you will need

Aprons

Plastic food models or food pictures

Cash drawer, play cash register, or cigar box

Play money

Shopping bags (paper or plastic)

Words you can use

shop	grocery
money	taste
more	supermarket
aisle	buy
like	dislike
store	manager
owner	vegetables
fruits	meat
milk	eggs
yogurt	

other food words

napkins	paper cups
toilet paper	shampoo
soap	

laundry detergent

other nonfood words

bag	paper
plastic	delivery
truck	customer
shopper	

amounts of money

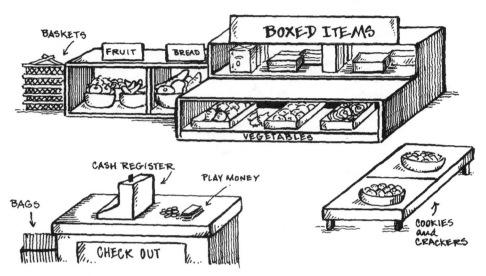

What to do

- Encourage the children to play the roles of the storeowners, employees, and shoppers.
- If necessary, facilitate their play by providing materials for the store or by acting as a shopper.
- The children will shop, ask for certain foods, and go through the "checkout counter." Let them select the roles that they will play, and let the activity evolve as the children desire.
- While shopping the children will use descriptive language as they communicate what they want (both food and nonfood items) and how much they need.
- Play money and a cash register enrich this activity and add an additional stimulus for both receptive and expressive language.
- If appropriate, add the roles of the farmer, delivery person, etc.

Questions to assess language development

EXPRESSIVE LANGUAGE

Can children name (label) the foods/items in the market?

Can children model language used in the grocery store?

RECEPTIVE LANGUAGE

Can children identify foods/items by the label?

Literacy Connections

READING EXPERIENCES

Feast for 10 by Cathryn Falwell
> This is a beautiful counting book that tells the story of a family shopping for groceries and making dinner.

Market! by Ted Lewin
> Follow along and see how goods are bought and sold in faraway market places.

Tommy at the Grocery Store by Bill Grossman
> When Tommy the pig gets left behind at a grocery store, he is mistaken for various groceries, including salami, a potato, and a banana. Finally, his mother comes to save him.

- Have food ads from the newspaper available in the dramatic play center and the reading center.
- Have empty food cartons available in the dramatic play center.

WRITING EXPERIENCES

- Invite children to write or dictate signs, ads, and other printed items usually seen in grocery stores.
- Have blank books or story paper available for children to write about their shopping trips with their families.

Telephone Time

Children love to pretend to talk on the telephone, whether they are receiving or making calls in their play. With the advent of the cellular phone, children now can play telephone in just about any setting imaginable.

What you will need

Toy telephone(s)

Words you can use

greetings: hello, good-bye

telephone

dial tone

receiver

busy

signal

mouthpiece

talk

cellular

loud

soft

manners

make

receive

call

pretend

real

make believe

answer

ear

mouth

ringing

rotary

dial

touch

What to do

● Show the children a telephone and demonstrate how it is used. Most children have observed their parents and others using the telephone so this step may not be necessary. If it is, show them which end is placed against the ear and which end is the mouthpiece.

● Ask them how they know when someone is calling. Discuss their answers.

● Ask them what they think they should say when they answer the phone and when they are finished talking on the phone. This is an excellent opportunity to talk about good manners and politeness.

● Places the telephone(s) in the dramatic play center and let the children take it from there.

● If you decide to play, you can suggest people to call—mom, dad, grandmother, grandfather, sister, brother, boss, grocery store—to start conversations. One play telephone is sufficient, but should two be available, the children can call and chat with each other.

More

Use a real telephone to demonstrate dial tone and busy signals.

Questions to assess language development

EXPRESSIVE LANGUAGE

Can children model the correct way to answer the telephone?

Can children name the different parts of the telephone?

RECEPTIVE LANGUAGE

Can children correctly dial telephone numbers they are given?

Literacy Connections

READING EXPERIENCES

Grandpa Bud by Siophan Dodds

Polly calls Grandpa Bud on the telephone to request snacks for each of her stuffed animals coming to his sleepover.

Martha Speaks by Susan Meddaugh

A dog named Martha learns to speak by eating alphabet soup, and then puts her skills to good use on the telephone.

WRITING EXPERIENCES

● Place a note pad and pen beside the telephone in the dramatic play center. Model and encourage children to use the pad to take messages.

● Get permission from parents for children to share telephone numbers. Make blank "telephone books." Let children write each classmate's name and telephone number on a page. Depending on the understanding of the children, pages can be alphabetized or not. Be sure to check each child's book for accuracy before sending it home.

● If a phone book of real phone numbers is not acceptable, have children make pretend phone books to use in the dramatic play center.

I'll Be the Mommy...

Children often explore family roles in their play. Family roles are some of the first symbolic play milestones children reach. They love to enact familiar family routines, particularly those marking special events. As they pretend to be different family members, the children talk and act out various roles.

What you will need

Provide a variety of props such as old clothing (male and female, adult and child) such as shoes, jackets, hats, ties

Telephone

Chairs

Empty food containers

Dishes, pots, pans

Doll, beds, toys, and baby clothes

Words you can use

mom	dad
baby	children
house	home
play	inside
outside	toys
breakfast	lunch
dinner	meals
bedtime	naptime
grocery store	shopping
get dressed	pants
shirts	socks
shoes	dress
sweater	coat
mittens	gloves
hat	

What to do

- Designate an area of the room as the housekeeping center.
- Children will gravitate to and play in this center with little direction. However, you might suggest a situation, such as preparing for the baby's first birthday party; getting ready to go to the child care center; going to Grandma's and Grandpa's home; and getting ready to take a trip in the car, bus, train, or plane.

What you will need

EXPRESSIVE LANGUAGE

Can the children use words appropriate to the roles they are creating?

RECEPTIVE LANGUAGE

Do the children show an understanding of the different language and voices used to represent various family members?

Literacy Connections

READING EXPERIENCES

Daddies by Adele Aron Greenspan
  A prose poem about daddies—what they do, teach, and give. Illustrated with black and white photos.

Octopus Hug by Laurence Pringle
  Since Mom has gone out for the evening, Dad plays with the kids in daddy-style roughhouse play.

This Quiet Lady by Charlotte Zolotow
  A young girl looks at her collection of photos and points out her mother during different stages of her life, from childhood to mother-to-be.

What Will Mommy Do When I'm at School? by Dolores Johnson
  A young girl is afraid of starting school and leaving mom at home to do all the chores by herself. Mom reassures the girl that she's going to be fine, since she's starting a new job.

WRITING EXPERIENCES

- Make available a wide variety of writing materials, including recipe cards, paper for shopping lists and telephone messages, stationery and envelopes, and so on.

- Have small blank books available for children to create books about their families. Children can draw illustrations then write or dictate stories about their families.

- To help children understand the many varieties of families, encourage children to draw pictures of their families doing something. After writing or dictating captions for their drawings, help them hang their illustrations in a special family display. Read the captions and encourage children to read them.

Clothes Have Names Too

This activity helps children acquire the descriptive vocabulary of clothing that they wear daily as well as the dress-up clothing in the housekeeping area.

What you will need

A few of the following props: socks, shoes, hat, pants, shirt, sneakers, dress, coats, jacket, boots, sandals, pajamas, underpants, undershirt, skirt, jeans, bib, apron, belt, suspenders, tie, ribbon.

Words you can use

socks

shoes

hat

pants

shirt

sneakers

dress

coat

jacket

boots

sandals

pajamas

underpants

undershirt

skirt

jeans

bib

apron

belt

suspenders

tie

ribbons

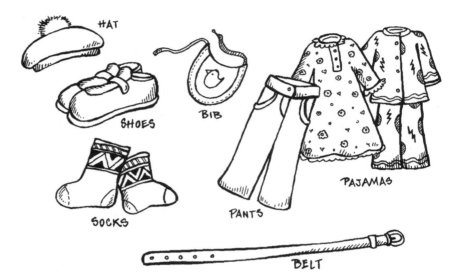

What to do

- Place an adequate supply of clothing items in the housekeeping area. Be sure they represent various roles that the children might play.
- Collect a number of clothing items from the housekeeping center. There should be at least one or two items of clothing for each child.
- Place the collection in the center of a circle formed by the children.
- Each child picks a piece of clothing and names it. If a child does not know the name of the item, then the others can help.
- If appropriate, ask the children how the clothing is used.

More

Take a specific clothing item. Let the children name specific parts of the clothing, such as a zipper, button, snap, fastener, sleeve, or collar.

Share clothing items from various professions that might be represented in the dress-up or housekeeping area, such as a police officer, letter carrier, pilot, doctor, or nurse.

Questions to assess language development

ESPRESSIVE LANGUAGE

Can children name (label) various pieces of clothing?

RECEPTIVE LANGUAGE

Can children identify clothing pieces by name?

Literacy Connections

READING EXPERIENCES

Aaron's Shirt by Deborah Gould
Aaron's favorite shirt is finally too small to wear, but just right to be handed down to his teddy bear.

The Dress I'll Wear to the Party by Shirley Neitzel
A cumulative story written in rhyme and rebus lists all the clothes a little girl has to wear to get ready for the party.

Froggy Gets Dressed by Jonathan London
Every time Froggy goes out to play in the snow, he leaves off one item of clothing and has to go back in, get undressed and then redressed.

Mary Wore Her Red Dress and Henry Wore His Green Sneakers by Merle Peek
Eight animals on their way to a party illustrate different colors and different pieces of clothing. Based on an old folk song.

WRITING EXPERIENCES

- Have blank books available cut in shapes of various pieces of clothing. Children can draw, write, or dictate in such books as "The Shoe Book" and "The Shirt Book."

- Using pictures of children and adults in various types of clothing, make charts by writing the name of the piece of clothing and drawing a line from the name to the person wearing the clothing. With young children, do this with them; with older children, help them only if needed.

Wash Day

Children love to wash things and to sort things. This activity combines both on a pretend laundry day, and adds practice in sequencing skills.

What you will need

Washtub
Soap and water, optional
Washboard, optional
Clothesline
Clothespins
Clothing items for various
    people in a family

Words you can use

wash
dry
pants
shirt
diapers
scrub
clothespin
socks
underwear
undershirts
gloves
hats
dresses
clothesline
washtub
washboard

What to do

● Put clothing items for a variety of family members in the dramatic play area.

● Add a washtub for the children to "wash" the clothes. If possible, add soap and water and a washboard.

● String a clothesline in an out-of-the-way section of the dramatic play area and encourage the children to hang their clothes to dry with clothespins, sorting them by family member. For example, hang all the baby clothes together, all the "brother" clothes together, and so on. Children can name (label) the items as they hang the clothes.

● Encourage children to play this activity together so that they can practice taking turns and conversing.

Questions to assess language development

ESPRESSIVE LANGUAGE

Can children name (label) what is needed for laundry day?

Can children verbalize a sequence for laundry day?

RECEPTIVE LANGUAGE

Can children group clothes by some sort of association (baby clothes, red clothes, all socks, etc.)?

Literacy Connections

READING EXPERIENCES

Froggy Gets Dressed by Jonathan London

> This repetitive tale about dressing will make listeners laugh and laugh.

Mrs. McNosh Hangs Up Her Wash by Sarah Weeks

> This silly rhyming tale offers first-rate word play.

WRITING EXPERIENCES

- Innovate on the text of *Froggy Gets Dressed* or other predictable books by copying a repetitive phrase on a chart, chalk board, or dry erase board. Invite children to help change the text. Cover the original words with new words written on Post-it notes. Read the new text together. Repeat with new changes as appropriate. Read each new innovation and encourage children to read with you. If written on chart paper, innovations can be saved for children to read at later times.

- Label pictures of clothing items with the appropriate names. Using a large drawing of a dresser, invite children to put clothing items in the drawers by taping the labeled clothing item to the dresser drawer. Similar items should go in the same drawer. Encourage children to talk about why they put items where they did.

Hats

Want to have a fun day at school? This activity is one that you can take your hat off to.

What you will need

A variety of hats representative of various professions (ask the parents as well as organizations in the community to donate them)

Words you can use

hats

wear

job

people

weather

decorate

firefighter

letter carrier

doctor

librarian

baker

baseball player

construction worker

other job names

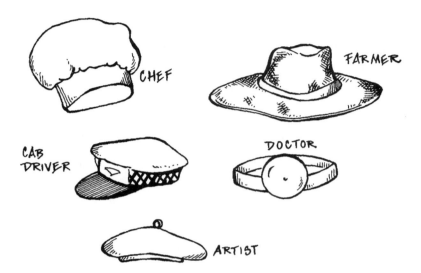

What to do

- Collect a variety of hats that represent various job roles that the children know about or can learn about through classroom visitors, books, and videos as well as their own personal experiences. A few examples include nurse, doctor, cook, police officer, letter carrier, farmer, baseball player, hockey player, construction worker, teacher, painter, cowboy or cowgirl, soldier.

- Let one child choose a hat and tell about the person she thinks might wear it.

- Encourage her to talk about why she chose this particular hat. Can she (by herself or with help from the other children) tell what kind of work a person wearing this hat might do?

- Ask the children what kind of hats they wear and why they wear them, such as safety helmets, rain hats, stocking caps, ball caps, shower caps.

More

Ask the parents and grandparents of the children to bring their favorite hat to school and share why they like it so much.

Make hats with the children from old newspapers. Let them decorate
them with scrap cloth material, beads, and old buttons. Ask them to
describe what their hat is for.

Questions to assess language development

ESPRESSIVE LANGUAGE

Can the children name (label) the person who wears a particular hat?

Can the children tell why they picked a particular hat?

Can the children tell about the person they are representing by their
particular hat?

RECEPTIVE LANGUAGE

Can the children make the association between a hat and the person
who might be wearing that hat?

Literacy Connections

READING EXPERIENCES

Hats for Sale by Esphyr Slobodkina

This is a lively tale of a peddler, some monkeys, and their monkey
business. It is a fun story to dramatize.

The Night Ones by Patricia Grossman

Many people work at night. This book explores careers such as
baker, office cleaner, and more.

Whose Hat? by Margaret Miller

Color photos of hats used in various jobs are paired up with photos
of adults and children dressed for the occupation. *Guess Who* and
Whose Shoe are similar books by the same author.

WRITING EXPERIENCES

● Have blank books available for the children to make books about
occupations they like. Titles might be "When I Grow Up" and
"Going to Work."

● Have children display the hats they usually wear. Make graphs about
the hats, such as "Colors of Our Hats" and "Words on Our Hats."

● Make a class book. Invite children to draw pictures of their family
members at work. Take dictation about their pictures and assemble
into a book. Read to the children, then place the book in the class
library.

● Invite children to create hat riddles. They can draw a hat and write
or dictate clues about who wears the hat. On the second page they
can draw and write the answer.

First Aid Station

This pretend play activity allows children to take on the role of health care professional and to expand their vocabulary by naming parts of the body, first aid equipment, and so on.

What you will need

A few of the following props: stethoscope, tongue depressors, cotton balls, bandages, thermometers, pressure cuff, nurse's hat, slings, gloves, notepad, pencils, clipboards. Use real items if they are safe for children to use, toy versions of items, or homemade versions of the items.

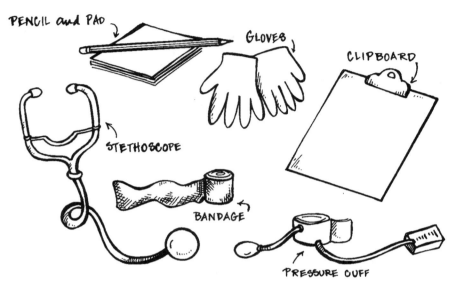

PENCIL and PAD

GLOVES

CLIPBOARD

STETHOSCOPE

BANDAGE

PRESSURE CUFF

Words you can use

fever	cut
sore throat	earache
scrape	headache
scratch	head
neck	arm
leg	torso
knee	mouth
throat	ear
eye	

other parts of the body

stethoscope

tongue depressors

cotton balls

bandages

thermometers

pressure cuff

nurse's hat

slings

gloves

What to do

- Set up an area of the classroom as a first aid center.
- Children choose a role as a health care professional or a patient, or they can bring in their doll or stuffed animal for care. Include props to encourage emerging literacy, such as notepad and pencils.
- Join the children by supporting their play and assisting them as needed in naming first aid equipment, injury, or ailment.
- If appropriate, expand this activity to include an ambulance and emergency room.

Questions to assess language development

ESPRESSIVE LANGUAGE

Can the children name (label) the items in a first aid station?

Can the children describe injuries or sicknesses in terms of parts of the body, how they hurt, and so on?

RECEPTIVE LANGUAGE

Can the children identify items in a first aid station?

Literacy Connections

READING EXPERIENCES

The Bear's Toothache by David McPhail

A boy dreams that a bear with a toothache is moaning in pain outside his bedroom window. The boy figures out a way to pull out the bear's tooth and gets to keep it as his reward.

The Checkup by Helen Oxenbury

Tells how a little boy feels about all the instruments in a doctor's office.

My Doctor by Harlow Rockwell

Explains each instrument the doctor uses and how it works.

My First Doctor Visit by Julia Allen

This book introduces children to the instruments and procedures of a doctor's office.

WRITING EXPERIENCES

- Have writing props available during play time. Include prescription pads, checks, and message pads. While joining in the play, model the use of the props and encourage children to use them.

- Create a chart of safety rules. As children talk about ways to be safe in the room, outside, at home, and in other places, write their words on chart paper. Hang the charts in the room and refer to them regularly.

Pet Shop

This child-initiated activity allows children to play out the roles in a pet shop, while practicing categorizing skills.

What you will need

Stuffed animals

Miniature animals

All types of pet supplies (food, bowls, leashes, hamster trails, aquarium, dog toys, cat toys)

Words you can use

dog

cat

puppy

kitten

fish

hamster

gerbil

guinea pig

ferret

horse

fish bowl

aquarium

cat food

dog food

bowl

leash

collar

toys

supplies

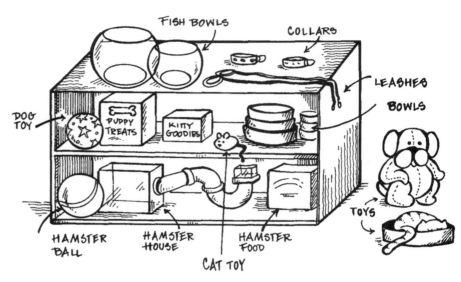

What to do

● Set up a pretend pet shop, including stuffed animals, feed bowls, water bowls, different types of pet foods, fish bowls, hamster trails, or leashes.

● Encourage the children to play in this area, occasionally prompting them with what items are appropriate for certain kinds of pets. For example, would a customer with a dog be looking for fish food?

● Let the play continue in this manner, perhaps encouraging children to categorize pet items appropriately.

Questions to assess language development

ESPRESSIVE LANGUAGE

Can children name (label) a variety of pets?

Can children name (label) items that are associated with particular pets in the pet shop?

RECEPTIVE LANGUAGE

Can children associate appropriate items with the pets for which they are intended?

Literacy Connections

READING EXPERIENCES

Herbie Hamster, Where Are You? by Terence Blacker

A pet hamster escapes form his cage.

I Really Want a Dog by S. Blakemore and S. Breslow

A boy imagines what fun he would have with a dog, and the responsibilities he would have taking care of the dog.

Michael and the Cats by Barbara Abercrombie

While Michael is visiting his aunt and uncle, he learns how to take care of their cats. They make friends with him when he learns how to treat them.

No Plain Pets! by Marc Barasch

A young boy wants an unusual pet and thinks about all the pets he could have.

Scruffy by Peggy Parish

A young boy learns how to choose and take care of his new pet cat.

● Collect brochures about animal care from pet stores or veterinarians. Have the brochures available in the dramatic play center or the class library.

WRITING EXPERIENCES

● Help children make signs for the Pet Shop.

● Have small blank books available for children to write or dictate books about animal care. If possible, arrange with a local veterinarian to place the finished books in the clinic.

● Invite children to make posters to list proper care for the class pets. Display the posters near the appropriate animal. Refer to the posters when the animal needs feeding, cleaning, and so on.

Beach Party

This role-play activity includes planning what to take to the beach, how to use these items at the beach, things that you can do at the beach, and descriptive words appropriate to the beach.

What you will need

Chart paper and marker or paper and markers

A few of the following props: beach towels, suntan lotion, goggles, beach ball,

Frisbee, flippers, sunglasses, beach hats, floats, inner-tubes, boogie boards, cooler, juice boxes, sand toys

Words you can use

beach

water

ocean

lake

river

towel

ball

goggles

sunglasses

suntan lotion

sunburn

beach hat

flippers

floats

swim

dig

play

bucket

shovel

sand

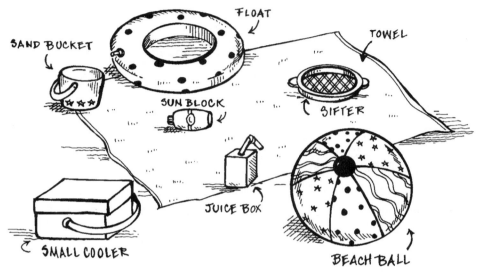

What to do

- Announce to the children that they are going to plan a "beach party." Encourage them to talk about the sorts of things they would take to a beach party. List these on chart paper, or the children can draw "list" pictures.
- Assemble the items needed. If desired, send a note home asking parents to send in items.
- Take the items to a designated spot in the classroom and pretend to have a beach party.
- Unpack, play beach games, and act out activities.

More

Incorporate snack time or fishing into the beach party.

Questions to assess language development

ESPRESSIVE LANGUAGE

Can children name (label) items appropriate to a beach party?

Can children describe beach environments in a conversation?

RECEPTIVE LANGUAGE

Can children identify items appropriate to a beach party?

Literacy Connections

READING EXPERIENCES

A Beach Day by Douglas Florian
   Simple text reveals the pleasures of a trip to the beach.

Harry by the Sea by Gene Zion
   Harry the dog gets caught in a sudden wave and is covered with sea-weed. All along the beach, the mysterious looking creature causes havoc.

Just Grandma and Me by Mercer Mayer
   A young boy has an enjoyable trip to the beach alone with his grandmother.

WRITING EXPERIENCES

- Involve the children in writing the note home requesting beach items.

- Take photos of the children at the "beach." Children can write or dictate captions for photos to be put in a book or scrapbook, or display on a wall.

- Encourage children to draw or paint pictures of their beach experiences. Invite the children to turn the picture over and write or dictate a postcard to someone in another class or a family member.

Shadow Creatures

Children use their imaginations to create and name (label) pretend animals from shadow creatures.

What you will need

Flashlight
Wall

Words you can use

dog
cat
pig
horse
cow
duck
rabbit
dear
bird
fish
goat
whale
dinosaur

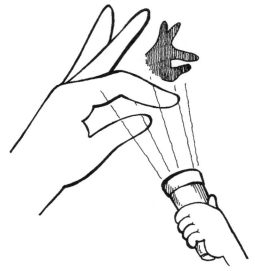

What to do

- Turn off the classroom lights.
- One child holds the flashlight while you make a shadow creature with your hands. This does not have to be a real animal; whatever you can make with your hands will do.
- The children take turns naming the shadow creature by using animal names they know or by combining animal names to make up new labels, such as using "rabdear" for a shadow creature that looks like a rabbit and dear.
- Give each child a turn to create shadow creatures as the other children guess or make up the names.

More

Use props instead of hands.
Use an overhead projector.

Questions to assess language development

Do children know animal names to call the shadow creatures?

Are children able to make up names for the various creatures?

Literacy Connections

READING EXPERIENCES

Bear Shadow by Frank Asch
> Bear wants to go fishing, but his shadow keeps scaring the fish away. He tries to get rid of his shadow in a number of ways.

Hanimations by Mario Mariotti
> Photos show one or two hands and forearms painted and arranged to resemble a variety of animals.

Henry and the Dragon by Eileen Christelow
> Henry is afraid of a shadow that looks very much like a dragon. He calls his parents in to investigate before he can go to bed.

I Have a Friend by Keiko Narahashi
> This is a simple story of a young boy who likes his shadow.

It Looked Like Spilt Milk by Charles G. Shaw
> White shapes are portrayed on blue backgrounds. Although the shapes take on familiar forms, the reader finds out at the end of the book that they are clouds.

WRITING EXPERIENCES

- Provide photos of shadows of various items. As children predict what makes the shadow, write down their words. Verify their predictions by showing the object.

- Measure children's shadows at different times throughout the day. Help children record the information in a shadow log book.

- On a piece of painting paper, have children drop blots of paint. While paint is still wet, fold paper in half. Open. Let children describe what their design looks like. Invite them to write or dictate captions for their shapes. Display the captioned art. Read the captions and encourage children to return to the pictures and read them.

Mommy and Daddy Helpers

Talking about the things that children can do to help their parents at home is an excellent way to teach them about the jobs that they can do at home and in school.

What you will need

Just imaginations

Words you can use

clean

wash

sweep

brush

pick up

help

cook

dress

job

toys

play

work

names of clothing items

What to do

● Ask the children to talk about the jobs they do at home to help their parents.

● Ask them to pretend they are just waking up and getting out of bed. They need to get ready to go to school. Are there things they can do to help their parents? Perhaps the children will say things like brushing their teeth, getting dressed, helping with breakfast, putting on coats, boots, etc.

● Ask them to pretend they are just getting home from school. What can they do to help their parents? The children may share ideas such as putting their coats away, picking up toys, and helping with meals.

● Encourage them to pretend that it is a day when they stay at home. What can they do to help their parents? How can they help when they go to a friend's home?

● Encourage the children to play being helpers in the dramatic play center.

More

Encourage the children to act out all the ways they can be helpful at home and in school.

Questions to assess language development

ESPRESSIVE LANGUAGE

Can children name (label) various tasks they see routinely performed at home?

Can children name (label) items associated with particular tasks/routines?

RECEPTIVE LANGUAGE

Can children replicate these task and routines with a sequence?

Can children identify items associated with particular tasks/routines?

Literacy Connections

READING EXPERIENCES

Daddy Makes the Best Spaghetti by Anna Grossnickle Hines

In this delightful book, family routines are transformed into joyful games.

Farm Morning by David McPhail

A father and daughter share the daily rituals of a farm morning.

Pig Pig Gets a Job by David McPhail

Pig Pig needs a job to earn some money. After considering jobs such as a cook, auto mechanic, and circus trainer, he finally decides to work around the house for pay.

WRITING EXPERIENCES

- Have small blank books available for children to write or dictate stories about how they help at home.

- Help children make graphs of how they help at home. For example, under the heading *I pick up my clothes,* children can write their names under *Yes* or *No.*

- Invite children to make a list of classroom chores. Use their list to determine classroom helpers.

- Encourage children to write or dictate letters to families suggesting ways they will help with household chores.

Where Do I Belong?

Categorizing things and learning how things are used are important skills for children to develop as they explore their environments. This activity gives children an opportunity to name items (some familiar and some not so familiar) and then to categorize them according to their use, place in the household, etc.

What you will need

A few of the following props: silverware, diapers, plates, rattles, jewelry, napkins, baby lotion, pots/pans, baby powder, high heels, dress, purse, empty makeup containers, and other items that can be categorized

GLASS

POT WITH LID

PLATE

PAN

SILVERWARE

BOWL

Words you can use

fork	knife
spoon	plate
glass	napkin
diapers	rattles
baby lotion	baby powder
pots	pans

mixing bowl

measuring cups

measuring spoons

jewelry

high heels

dress

purse

empty makeup containers

baby

mother

father

cooking

eating

What to do

● Set up a display of various items. These may include cooking items, baby clothes or items, bathroom items, and toiletry items.

● Encourage the children to name items individually, and then place them in a pile by "where" they go—baby's room, kitchen, bathroom.

More

Using a dollhouse, name and place the items in the correct location.

Act out the use of kitchen items, baby items, and other items.

Put items in one category and include one that doesn't belong. The children pick out the one that does *not* belong.

Questions to assess language development

ESPRESSIVE LANGUAGE

Can children name (label) the various items?

Can children say *why* items might belong in a certain grouping?

RECEPTIVE LANGUAGE

Can children identify various items by name?

Can children categorize the items by associating where they belong?

Literacy Connections

READING EXPERIENCES

Pots and Pans by Anne Rockwell

Two young children explore the kitchen and identify the different pots and pans they find.

The Old Woman Who Named Things by Cynthia Rylant

An old woman keeps from being lonely by naming the things in her life, like her house and her bed.

Where Does It Go? by Margaret Miller

Color photographs and silly questions invite participation in this funny book about where things belong.

● Create a Word Wall by gluing pictures of objects on poster board cards and writing the names of the objects beside them. Tape the words on the wall in category lists, such as clothes words, backyard words, and so on. Read the words regularly, and invite children to read them.

WRITING EXPERIENCES

● Have blank books and pictures of household items cut from catalogs available. Invite children to make books about different parts of their house by gluing appropriate pictures in their books and labeling the objects. For example, children might make a "Bedroom Book" by gluing in pictures of beds, dressers, and mirrors. Encourage them to write or dictate labels on each page.

What Does My Face Say?

Facial expression is one way to send a message to a person or persons. This activity lets children practice this "social use" of nonverbal language with a mirror. Reading the facial expression of others is as important as knowing what your face may be "saying."

What you will need

Mirror
List of facial expressions

Words you can use

happy
sad
brave
excited
mad
angry
scared
surprised
shy
face
mirror

What to do

- Ask the children to sit before a long mirror (a full-length mirror set sideways works well, as children can lie on the floor and see one another's faces in the mirror).
- Encourage all the children to make a "happy" face. Each child looks at his own face and all the other children's versions of "happy" faces.
- Ask them to make another kind of "happy" face. Again, each child looks at his face and all the other children's faces.
- Encourage them to make various "readable" faces, such as mad, scared, excited, surprised, or sad.

More

Children can pair up and read their partner's facial expressions.

Draw various "readable" faces, then try these faces.

Name an event or occasion, such as riding a roller coaster or attending a birthday party, and ask the children put on the "face" that goes with the event.

Make opposite faces such as happy/sad, excited/bored, and scared/brave.

Questions to assess language development

ESPRESSIVE LANGUAGE

Can children name (label) the various feelings that their face and others' faces are showing?

RECEPTIVE LANGUAGE

Can children understand the meaning of the various "face" words, such as happy, sad, or angry?

Can children match an expression word to the face they are seeing?

Literacy Connections

READING EXPERIENCES

I Like It When by Mary Murphy

A little penguin shares his feelings with his mother about the things he likes as they perform routine activities.

I Was So Mad by Norma Simon

Clear pictures and minimal text help children understand why they get angry and what they can do about it.

The Temper Tantrum Book by Edna Preston Mitchell

Children feel empathy for the angry animals in this story,

WRITING EXPERIENCES

● Take Polaroid pictures of the children making various faces. Glue each picture on a piece of paper. Invite each child to write or dictate information about what causes them to make such faces. Assemble into a class book. Read the book to the children, then place the book in the class library.

● Photocopy pictures of people with different expressions. Make individual books. Invite children to write or dictate about the pictures. Children can read their books to others and place them in the class library.

Where Do I Live?

This activity encourages children to develop advanced categorizing skills. Each child acts out an animal, and then the group says *where* that animal lives.

What you will need

List of animals and their natural habitats

Words you can use

jungle
elephant
tiger
antelope
monkey
snake
home
dog
cat
goldfish
hamster
gerbil
farm
cow
pig
horse
chicken
pony
forest
dear
chipmunk
birds
bear
wolf

What to do

● Sit in a circle.
● Each child takes a turn acting out an animal. If necessary, suggest animals for the children to act out.
● The group guesses the animal and determines one of the three places—jungle, farm, or forest—that it can live.
● Ask the children to sit together with the other jungle, farm, or forest animals.
● Encourage the children to play together as animals from the various habitats.

More

Change or extend the categories to be simpler or more complicated—rain forest, desert, zoo—depending on the abilities and needs of the children.

Draw the various habitats—zoo, farm, jungle—and use the drawings to expand the concept of categories.

Questions to assess language development

Can the children name (label) a variety of animals?

Can the children say where the various animals live?

Can the children name animals by category?

Literacy Connections

READING EXPERIENCES

Is Your Mama a Llama? by Deborah Guarino

> A little llama asks a series of animals the title question. Each animal describes its mother, helping the llama—and the reader—guess the rhyming answer.

A Nice Walk in the Jungle by Nan Bodsworth

> During a field trip through the jungle, Miss Jellaby's class is swallowed by a boa constrictor. The teacher rescues them all, but they get to see many jungle animals.

One Red Rooster by Kathleen Sullivan Carroll

> A counting book in rhyme, this book focuses on animals that live on the farm.

WRITING EXPERIENCES

- Invite children to write or dictate captions for their drawings about animal habitats. Display the captioned drawings. Read the captions to the children and encourage the children to refer to them.

- Using pictures of animals glued to blank pages, create class books. Children can dictate information about each of the animal's habitats.

- Invite children to write a letter to the zoo asking for information about animal habitats.

What Am I?

While hearing is a sense, listening is a skill that can be practiced. Children get to practice their listening skills, especially auditory discrimination, while enjoying this activity.

What you will need

Pictures of things that make a noise that a child can imitate, grouped by category

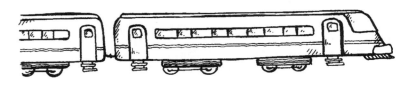

Words you can use

noise

sound

cow

horse

pig

dog

cat

car

train

bus

airplane

truck

boat

drum

bells

triangle

rhythm blocks

maracas

tambourine

What to do

● Gather together pictures of any noise-making items from one category, such as animals, transportation, or musical instruments. (Use pictures of things in more than one category after the children have done this activity a few times.)

● Give each child in the group a picture, instructing them not to show it to anyone else.

● The children then take turns making the noise or sound of their pictured item while the others guess *what* they are.

● The children verify guesses by showing their hidden pictures.

Questions to assess language development

ESPRESSIVE LANGUAGE

Can children name (label) the item that is making the noise?

RECEPTIVE LANGUAGE

Can children identify the noise they are hearing?

Literacy Connections

READING EXPERIENCES

All the Way Home by Lore Segal

Little Juliet falls down on a trip to the park and cannot be comforted. Written as a cumulative story, it includes many noises for readers to imitate, including crying, barking, and meowing.

Good-Night, Owl! by Pat Hutchins

Owl is trying to sleep, but all the animals are keeping him awake with their noises. When it gets dark, and all the other animals fall asleep, owl wakes them with his screeching.

Let's Go Home, Little Bear by Martin Waddell

On their walk through a snowy wood, Little Bear relies on Big Bear's reassurance that all the noises he hears are normal and nothing to fear.

WRITING EXPERIENCES

● Have small books available for children to write about sounds in their lives. For example, books may be titled "Sounds in the Classroom" or "Sounds in My House." Help them write, dictate, or draw things that make noises such as "The clock makes a tick-tick sound."

● Children might write sound riddles. Invite them to write or dictate clues describing sounds made by a variety of objects. They can read their riddles to other children on their own or during circle time.

I Am...

This activity develops dramatic play skills, expressive language, sequencing skills, and memory skills—and the children have a good time, too!

What you will need

Props related to one of the sample activities listed below

Words you can use (sample activities)

getting dressed

setting the table

getting ready for bed

eating supper/lunch

making a sandwich

coloring a picture

putting on your shoes

brushing your teeth

taking the dog for a walk

playing house

playing school

any pretend activity

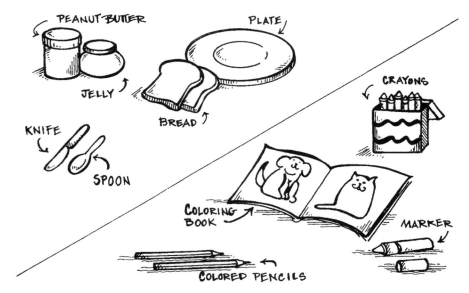

What to do

- Pick out daily activities that are fun and familiar to the children. Simple routines from home and school are best.
- Tell one child, "Show me how to . . . "
- One child acts out the activity first, saying the steps he is showing. For example, for making a sandwich: get the bread, get the peanut butter, etc.

More

Ask one child to describe what another child is doing as he does it.

Have one child tell another the steps he must do to pretend an activity. For example, for going to sleep: put your head down, close your eyes, etc.

Questions to assess language development

ESPRESSIVE LANGUAGE

Can children say *what* they are doing as they act out a daily activity?

RECEPTIVE LANGUAGE

If one child is acting out, while another child describes the activity, can the child who is acting out the activity understand what he needs to do?

Can children describe the activity in a "correct" sequence?

Literacy Connections

READING EXPERIENCES

At the Laundromat by Christine Loomis
One of a series of *In the Neighborhood* books, this book is filled with the familiar sight and sounds of the laundromat. Other books in the series include *At the Library, At the Mall,* and *In the Diner.*

Just for You by Mercer Mayer
Little Critter tries to help his mother by doing things such as putting away the dishes, carrying in the groceries, and setting the table, but each attempt ends in less than helpful conclusions. Other Mercer Mayer books involve Little Critter in a variety of daily routines.

What's What? A Guessing Game by Mary Serfozo

What is hard or soft? What is dark or light? These questions are answered in rhyme.

● Use a sequence of photos or drawings of people involved in familiar routines. On a line tied between two chairs, hang the illustrations in the proper sequence. Invite children to hang illustrations of other actions in sequence. Talk about the actions while placing them on the line.

WRITING EXPERIENCES

● On a chart or in a small book, help children write directions for making simple things, such as a peanut butter sandwich. Provide the materials for them to complete the task, referring to the directions.

● Invite children to write lists of things to do in the center. For example, they might make a list of things to do at clean-up time. Post their lists and refer to them at appropriate times.

Outdoor Play

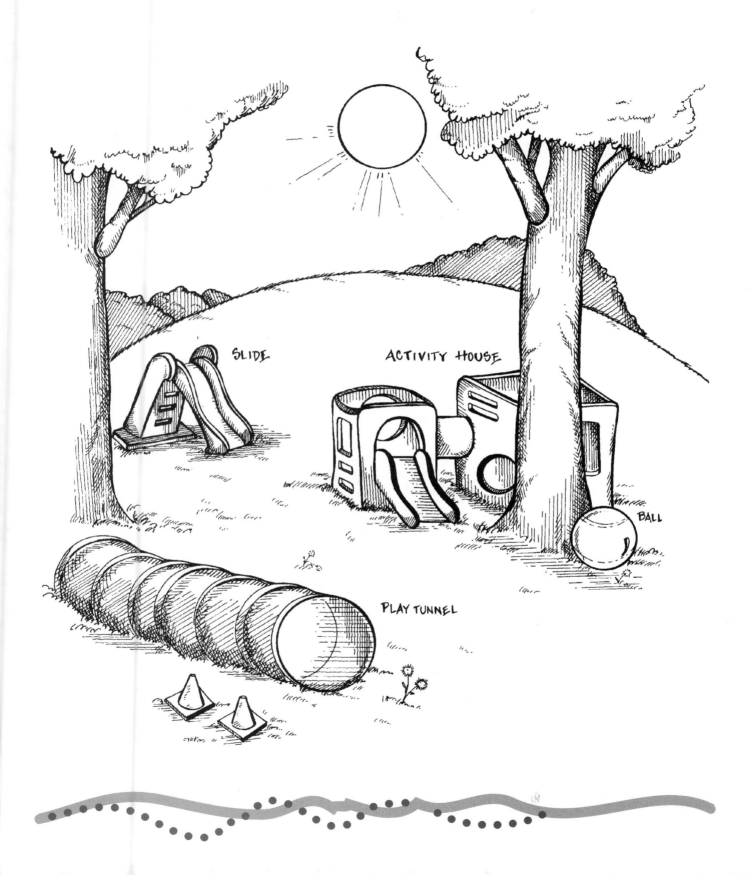

SLIDE

ACTIVITY HOUSE

BALL

PLAY TUNNEL

Parachutes

Playing with parachutes is the perfect way to practice turn-taking and expressive language.

What you will need

Nylon parachute

Words you can use

parachute
use
down under
soft
waves
jump
slow
fall
high
fast
land
bend
hard
soft
low

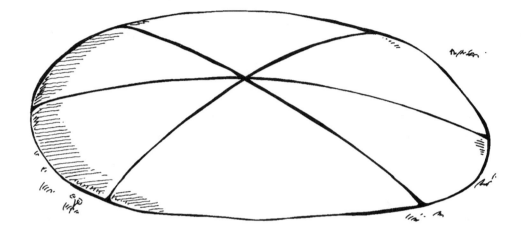

What to do

- Take a group of children and the nylon parachute outside.
- Everyone stands around the edge of the parachute, spaced evenly, and holds an edge of a handle.
- Grab the edge; flap the parachute up, trapping air in the parachute, then let the air out.
- Make tiny waves with the parachute by waving arms up and down.
- One or two children can let go of the parachute and go under it as the rest of the group lifts the parachute up. Try this with the whole group lifting the parachute, letting go of it, then running under it before it falls down on them (but not on a windy day).
- Put the parachute away, and begin pretending. Ask the children if they've ever seen someone jump from a plane and use a parachute to come down.
- Demonstrate a jump, a pull of the ripcord of the parachute, and a slow falling motion through the air.
- The children each take a turn being the "parachute" person.

More

Expand various roles, such as the airplane pilot. Use picture cues, if necessary.

Incorporate jumps from various heights, such as from a curb or low benches. Supervise closely.

Questions to assess language development

RECEPTIVE LANGUAGE

Can children pretend the sequence being described?

Can children follow the directions to manipulate the parachute in a large group?

Literacy Connections

READING EXPERIENCES

First Flight by David McPhail

A little boy takes his teddy on an airplane ride but Teddy misbehaves.

Into This Night We Are Rising by Jonathon London

Children have an adventure by flying through the night sky. They later safely return to their beds.

Rainy Day Dream by Michael Chesworth

A little boy is swept up with his umbrella and flies over the countryside.

Tomorrow, Up and Away! by Pat L. Collins

A turtle wishes to fly, and his wish comes true. However, in the end, he is not happy with it.

The Wing Shop by Elvira Woodruff

Matthew wants to get back to the street where he used to live, so he tries out a variety of wings in an attempt to fly.

WRITING EXPERIENCES

- Have small blank books available with titles such as "My Airplane Trip" and "Things That Fly." Invite children to draw, write, or dictate their stories about objects that fly.

- Make a chart of "Things That Fly." Divide the chart in half, labeling one column "Living Things" and the other "Non-living Things." Ask the children to list things to write on the chart, helping them decide which column to write in.

I Love a Parade

This activity involves the use of dress-up clothing and spatial relationships in a fun and interactive way that challenges children to use descriptive words (expressive language).

What you will need

Dress-up items for a parade

Words you can use

first

second

third

middle

last

hat

boa

scarf

purse

handbag

gloves

walking stick

march

parade

start

stop

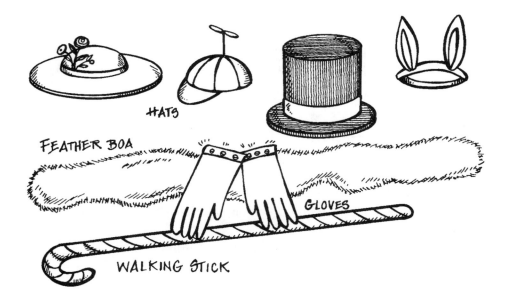

What to do

● Gather hats, gloves, scarves, boas, purses, and walking sticks. Make them available to the children so that they can dress up for the parade.

● Ask the children to line up, mentioning *first, second, middle, last*, and any other spatial relationship terms that may be appropriate.

● The children parade around a designated area, either inside or out.

● Periodically change the position of each child in the parade so that they can experience different spatial relationships.

● Ask the children to describe to the group the items that they have chosen and why they chose them.

Questions to assess language development

EXPRESSIVE LANGUAGE

Can children name their dress-up items?

Can children say "why" they chose certain items?

Do children understand the spatial terms *first* and *last?*

Do children understand other spatial terms such as *second* and *third?*

Literacy Connections

READING EXPERIENCES

The Jacket I Wear in the Snow by Shirley Neitzel

> A cumulative verse that tells the story of a child who gets her scarf stuck in her jacket zipper.

Shoes From Grandpa by Mem Fox

> When Jessie gets shoes from grandpa, her family buys her a whole new outfit to go with them. Written in the cumulative style of "The House That Jack Built." Children will soon chant the refrain.

There's a Party at Mona's Tonight by Harry Allard

> Potter Pig gets kicked out of Mona's party. He tries to get back in by dressing in different costumes, including a statue and Santa Claus.

WRITING EXPERIENCES

● Help children write signs that label who they are in a parade. For example, signs might say "Clown" or "Horn Player." Hang the signs around the children's necks and let them parade around the yard.

● As children plan their parade, help them write a list of the order of performers. Refer to the list when lining up.

● Have small blank books available at the writing center for children to write in about parades.

Listening Parade

This activity targets the auditory skill of discriminating loudness, and it also helps children to focus in on meaningful and pretend gestures.

What you will need

Musical instruments that can be carried (see Funky Junky Music, page 178)

Noisemakers

Words you can use

loud

quiet

noisy

little

soft

low

high

big

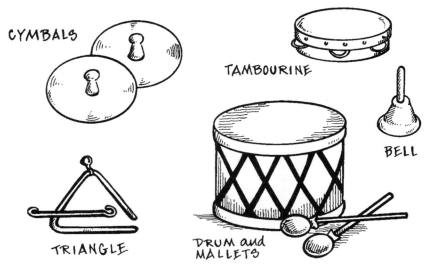

What to do

- Tell the children that they are going to have a "listening" parade. Ask the children to put on their "listening ears" and follow directions for loud vs. quiet playing. Tell them to listen for verbal cues and watch for gestural cues.
- Each child gets an instrument and falls into line.
- Tell them to play loud while making a hand gesture going up. The parade begins and the children play loud.
- Continue leading the parade, and tell them to play quietly while making a hand gesture going down.
- Alternate loud and quiet play.
- The children can take turns giving the "loud" and "quiet" cues.

Questions to assess language development

EXPRESSIVE LANGUAGE

Can children give the directions for loud and quiet sounds?

Can children call "loud" noises by another term?

Can children call "quiet" noises by another term?

RECEPTIVE LANGUAGE

Can children follow the directions for loud and quiet sounds?

Literacy Connections

READING EXPERIENCES

Listen to the Rain by Bill Martin, Jr. and John Archambault

All the sounds and silences of the rain are brought to the ear in this lyrical book. From the whispers to the "sounding, pounding roaring rain" the rhythm of the words and the striking illustrations help readers listen to the rain.

The Listening Walk by Paul Showers

A little girl takes a listening walk with her father and dog. They hear loud, soft, mechanical, and animal sounds on their walk.

What Noise? by Debbie MacKinnon and Anthea Sieveking

Photos of toddlers with their pets and toys illustrate the many sounds in a child's world.

Zin! Zin! Zin!: A Violin by Lloyd Moss

This counting book is an interesting introduction to musical instruments. From a trombone solo to the entire orchestra, instruments are added making duets, trios, and so on.

WRITING EXPERIENCES

● Have blank books available for children to illustrate things that make loud and soft sounds. Invite children to write about the items or take dictation for them.

● Make a class chart of "Loud Sounds" and "Quiet Sounds."

Teddy Bear Picnic

Role-playing allows children to recreate activities from their lives. Developing expressive language and social language are the goals in this developmentally appropriate pretend scheme.

What you will need

A few of the following props: plates, cups, spoons, water, teddy bears, picnic blanket, picnic basket, cookies (or snack)

Words you can use

picnic

spoons

plates

cups

teddy bears

picnic blanket

picnic basket

water

please

thank you

bugs

pour

likes

does not like

pass

play

What to do

● Send a note home a few days prior to the event, asking parents to send a teddy bear to school with the child on the chosen date.

● On the day of the teddy bear picnic, the children bring their teddy bears to school. (Be sure to have a few extra bears in case a child forgets to bring one in.)

● Ask the group what they need for a picnic, encouraging the children to name and gather picnic items.

● Go outside with the teddy bears and the picnic items.

● Hold a teddy bear picnic, modeling how to take turns and use good manners.

● Name picnic foods and say whether teddy "likes" or "does not like" certain items.

More

Extend the pretend picnic sequence in any manner the children prefer. Teddies can make friends with other teddies, can baby-sit for smaller teddies, etc.

The children can pretend to be teddy bears after the picnic meal and engage in outdoor play.

Take the picnic to a nearby park.

Questions to assess language development

EXPRESSIVE LANGUAGE

Are the children able to produce politeness markers, such as "please, thank you, please pass the _____?"

RECEPTIVE LANGUAGE

Are children able to pretend at the picnic sequence?

Literacy Connections

READING EXPERIENCES

Picnic by Emily A. McCully

In this wordless picture book, a family of mice don't notice that Baby mouse has fallen off the truck until they start their picnic.

It's the Bear by Jez Alborough

When the big bear interrupts the picnic, Eddie hides in the picnic basket. The bear eats all the goodies while Eddie and his mother run away.

The Rattlebang Picnic by Margaret Mahy

The McTavishes pack for a picnic near a hot spring. Soon the mountain jiggles and rumbles and the volcano blows, making more than their old car rattle and bang.

WRITING EXPERIENCES

- Help children write invitations to their teddy bears, inviting them to the picnic.
- On chart paper, make a class list of items they will need for the picnic.
- Help children write thank you notes from their teddy bears.

Egg Hunt

Naming colors and answering *where* questions are the primary objectives of this activity. The hunt is so much fun, and it can be done at any time of the year.

What you will need

Plastic eggs

Words you can use

color words

location words such as under, in front of, next to, on top of, on, behind, between

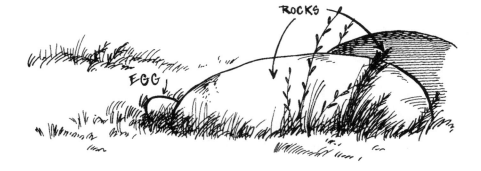

What to do

- Hide the eggs outdoors.
- Gather all the children together in one spot.
- Tell the children to find two eggs, to remember where they found them, and to come back to where they started.
- The children search for their eggs and after finding them return to the spot where they started.
- Each child then takes a turn telling the color of one egg he found and *where* he found it. Then each child gets another turn to tell the color of the second egg and *where* he found it.

More

Ask older children to find and describe more than two eggs.

Split the children into two groups; one group hides the eggs, and the other group finds the eggs.

On special occasions, put something inside the plastic eggs, such as tiny hearts or candy on Valentine's Day.

Questions to assess language development

Can children name the color of their eggs?

Can children name the location where they found their eggs? Do they need prompts to answer *where* questions? If so, what types of prompts seem to work best?

RECEPTIVE LANGUAGE

Can children show where they found their eggs?

Literacy Connections

READING EXPERIENCES

The Best Easter Egg Hunt Ever by John Speirs

The children in the story are going on an Easter egg hunt, and the reader is invited. Rebuses give clues as the reader searches the pages for hidden Easter treats.

Easter Egg Artists by Adrienne Adams

The Easter egg artists do a lot of decorating in this delightful picture book.

The Easter Egg Farm by Mary Jane Auch

A hen named Pauline begins to lay eggs with colors and designs. Just as the egg lady comes to pick up the eggs for an Easter egg hunt, they begin to hatch. As they grow, the chickens are as beautiful as their eggs.

WRITING EXPERIENCES

● Children can write or dictate special messages to be placed inside the plastic eggs before hiding them.

● Invite each child to hide an egg and write or dictate a clue to where it is hidden.

● Have blank books available in egg shapes. Children can draw and write or dictate egg stories.

Going Fishing

Children fish their way to learning about sequencing skills, naming skills, and comparison skills.

What you will need

Fishing poles (sticks)

String

Small magnets

Paper clips

Pictures of fish or paper, markers, and scissors

Words you can use

catfish

goldfish

angelfish

piranha

dogfish

shark

jellyfish

octopus

mermaid

dolphin

whale

blowfish

stingray

crab

clam

seashell

worms

pole

cricket

turtle

crocodile

alligator

What to do

- Attach strings to sticks. Tie a magnet at the end of each string.
- The children sit on a raised area, such as on railroad ties or a curb, or around a small plastic swimming pool.
- Put pictures of fish, each with a paper clip attached, in the pool or this recessed area. (Instead of pictures, the children can color and cut out the fish for the pool.)
- The children move their fishing poles around the pool or recessed area, looking for "fish."
- Encourage the children to say what kind of fish they have "caught," either naming (labeling) or describing it (by color, by size, and so on).

More

Put pictures of items other than fish into the "pool." For example, you might put in other water creatures, or junk (then you can talk about the environment).

Use a "fantasy" water adventure, with mermaids and mythical creatures.

Questions to assess language development

EXPRESSIVE LANGUAGE

EXPRESSIVE LANGUAGE

Can children name various kinds of fish?

Can children use descriptive words to say what their fish looks like?

RECEPTIVE LANGUAGE

Can children identify different kinds of "fish"?

Literacy Connections

READING EXPERIENCES

Fishing by Diana Engle

> Loretta loved spending the days fishing with Grandpa. When she and her mom move away, Loretta misses Grandpa until she finally goes fishing for—and catches—a new friend.

Fishing Sunday by Tony Johnson

> Going fishing with Grandfather, who always talks to the fish, is embarrassing. However, one fishing Sunday, the boy begins to see his grandfather in a new light.

Fishing with Dad by Michael J. Rosen

> The author recaptures all the Sundays he spent fishing with his father. All the details of a fishing trip are portrayed in lyric style.

McElligot's Pool by Dr. Seuss

> Written in classic Seuss rhyme, a boy imagines all the wild fish he could catch in McElligot's pool.

WRITING EXPERIENCES

- If there is an aquarium in the classroom, invite children to observe and describe the fish. They can write or dictate descriptions of the physical characteristics, as well as the behaviors, of the fish.

- Help children make a graph of the "fish" caught during the activity.

Let's Paint

As children move up, down, in, out, and pour or dip, they learn about spatial relationships.

What you will need

Paintbrushes

Buckets of water

Wall or fence to "paint"

Words you can use

up/down

wet/dry

messy

big/little

in/out

rough/smooth

splash

dip

pour

clean up

spill

paint

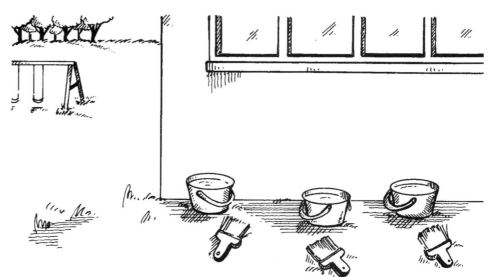

What to do

- Give each child a paintbrush. Set up several buckets of water nearby.
- The children dip their brushes into the water buckets to "paint" the outdoor wall or fence.
- Emphasize the concepts the children are using, such as brush in/out, bend up/down, paint up/down, wet/dry, etc.
- Talk about various surface concepts such as rough/smooth, big/little.

Questions to assess language development

EXPRESSIVE LANGUAGE

Can children name (label) actions, opposites, and adjectives from the above list (and others) as they "paint?"

RECEPTIVE LANGUAGE

Can children identify various terms as they are modeled in the activity?

Can children follow directions incorporating the terms from above?

Literacy Connections

READING EXPERIENCES

Mouse Paint by Ellen Walsh

Three white mice climb into jars of paint and come out different colors.

Oh, Were They Ever Happy! by Peter Spier

Three young children enjoy themselves on a painting spree when they paint their house in rainbow colors.

Over-Under by Catherine Matthias

Simply written, this book explains spatial relationships.

WRITING EXPERIENCES

- Invite children to write with water and small paintbrushes. They may want to write vanishing messages or practice single letters.

- Allow children to write with a variety of paints and papers. Put out tempera, watercolors, or fingerpaints. Encourage children to write messages in color. Also try writing with chalk or markers on wet paper, sandpaper, and other surfaces.

- Create a "graffiti wall" by taping a large sheet of blank paper on a wall. Have markers and crayons available for children to write and draw with.

Stop and Go

This action game helps children learn listening skills while practicing how to locate the source of a sound.

What you will need

Portable cassette tape player
Tapes of various types of music

Words you can use

music
start
stop
turn
listen
left
right
dance

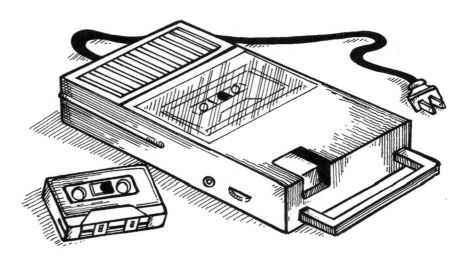

What to do

- The children line up side by side in a large group area (inside or out).
- Tell the children to "Turn to the side you hear the music on when it begins and dance until the music stops."
- Position yourself at either end of the line with a portable cassette tape player and turn the music on.
- The children turn to the direction of the music sound and dance until it stops.
- The children can take turns being the music player.

More

Expose children to various types of music, such as classical, rock, and reggae.

Questions to assess language development

RECEPTIVE LANGUAGE

Can children identify the source for the music?

Can they follow the direction to turn to the source of the music?

Can they begin with the music and stop with the music?

Literacy Connections

READING EXPERIENCES

Barn Dance by Bill Martin, Jr. and John Archambault

> A boy sneaks into the barn late one night and sees all the animals dancing. Written with strong rhythm and rhyme.

Dance Away by George Shannon

> Rabbit saves his friends from Fox by dancing away with a "left two three kick, right two three kick, left skip, right skip, turn around."

Hop Jump by Ellen Stoll Walsh

> Betsy the blue frog assures the green frogs that there's always room for dancing and hopping.

Max by Rachel Isodora

> Max is on his way to his baseball game. On the way, he warms up at his sister's ballet class.

WRITING EXPERIENCES

● Model how to make up a dance by writing directions like "Walk. Walk. Skip, skip, skip. Jump. Turn. Jump. Hop, hop, hop." Then help the children write directions for their own dances by taking their dictation on a chart. Some may want to write their own dances on paper. Let the children perform their dances while you read their directions to them.

● Children may want to perform their dances for others. Encourage them to write or dictate invitations to their performances. Other writing experiences could include creating simple programs, signs, tickets, and thank-you notes.

Red Light, Green Light

An old favorite, this game helps children learn auditory discrimination and color association, and practice following directions.

What you will need

Visual cues, if needed

Words you can use

red
green
yellow
stop
go
carefully
slowly
skip
hop
walk
run

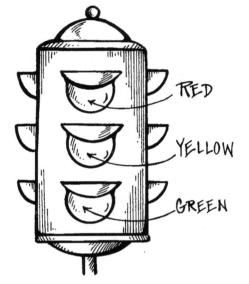

What to do

● Talk about how traffic lights work and what the signals mean. Emphasize that the green light means "go" and red light means "stop."

● The children form a line, standing next to one another.

● Stand in front of the line, facing the children.

● Call out "green light," and the children move toward you.

● Call out "red light," and the children stop.

● Play continues, with children associating "go" with green light and "stop" with red light.

● Let the children take turns calling out "green light" and "red light."

More

Use different movement patterns such as skipping or hopping for the next game.

Incorporate "yellow light" into the game, meaning "move slowly" or "move carefully."

Use visual cues, such as a green, red, or yellow paper circles.

Questions to assess language development

Do the children appear to be associating the colors with their meaning?

Can the children follow the directions according to their color association?

Literacy Connections

READING EXPERIENCES

The Farmer in the Dell by Ilse Plume

The familiar singing game is illustrated by the author.

Jeremy's Tail by Duncan Ball

Jeremy is blindfolded and playing pin the tail on the donkey at a birthday party. But before he can find the donkey, he ends up on a bus and has quite an adventure.

Playing Sardines by Beverly Major

The game of sardines is better than hide-and-seek. As each child finds the player who's "It," she must hide there, too, until everyone is scrunched together like a can of sardines.

WRITING EXPERIENCES

- Put out small blank books titled "Stop and Go" or "Red Light, Green Light." Encourage children to draw and write or dictate stories about things that stop and go.

- Make a class book about "Our Favorite Games." Each child can write or dictate and illustrate a page describing their favorite game. After reading the book to the class, put it in the class library.

- After playing a favorite class game, encourage children to draw or paint a picture of themselves playing with their friends. Have them write or dictate a caption for their picture. Put finished pictures on the wall or bulletin board. Use your finger to point to the words as you read the captions out loud. Encourage children to point to the captions and read also.

Falling Leaves Tree Match

A leaf-collecting walk encourages descriptive language about the color, shape, and size of leaves as well as the trees that they have fallen from.

What you will need

Collecting bags

Leaves from trees or from flowers, bushes, and other plants

Crayons and paper for rubbings

Words you can use

leaf
leaves
shape
tree
match
fall
fallen
big
little
small
tall
high
size
tiny
large
huge
texture
dry
brittle
soft
color names

What to do

- Give each child a collecting bag.
- Walk around the neighborhood or a nearby park and collect a variety of leaves.
- Examine the leaves. Try to locate the tree they have fallen from. Match the fallen leaves to those that are still on the trees.
- Talk about and compare the size, color, and texture of the leaves.
- After returning to the room, use the leaves for leaf rubbings or leaf pattern paintings.

More

Use a clear plastic shower curtain to make a leaf mural. Attach a variety of leaves to the curtain with masking tape. Turn the curtain over and use tempera paint to paint around the real leaf patterns.

Questions to assess language development

EXPRESSIVE LANGUAGE

Can children use descriptive words to describe the leaves that they find?

Can children name the trees that the leaves have fallen from?

RECEPTIVE LANGUAGE

Can children identify different trees and leaves as they are named?

Literacy Connections

READING EXPERIENCES

Red Leaf, Yellow Leaf by Lois Ehlert

> This delightful book tells about a sugar maple seed that takes root in the forest. After the young tree is gathered by nursery workers, a child helps plant it at home.

Why Do Leaves Change Color? by Betsy Maestro

> It's fall, and the leaves are changing color. This book explains the process of how leaves change color in autumn.

WRITING EXPERIENCES

- Help children label categories for the leaves they have found. They might write labels such as "red leaves" or "smooth leaves" on index cards and lay the leaves out beside the label, or glue labels and leaves on to large sheets of paper.

- Children could make name signs to place near the trees by writing or dictating the tree names on poster board. Staple poster board signs to wooden stakes and place near the trees they identify.

- Invite children to write or dictate letters to botanists at local universities or conservation offices describing leaves they have found and asking for help in identifying them.

Adventure Walk

Children can explore the language concepts of comparisons while taking a nature walk.

What you will need

Safe outdoor area
Leaves, grass, flowers, etc.

Words you can use

outside
flowers
leaves
rocks
grass
biggest/smallest
bigger/smaller
big/small

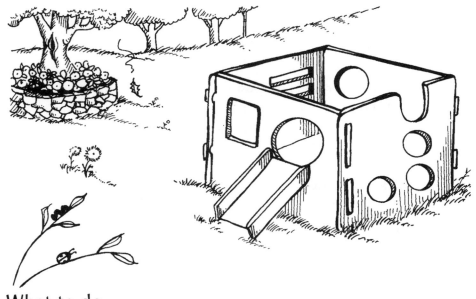

What to do

- Go for a walk outdoors.
- Encourage the children to look for things such as rocks, sticks, cans, bugs, grass, leaves, and flowers that are the same/different, big/bigger/biggest, small/smaller/smallest. Bring the things they found back to the classroom in a paper bag and then discuss and examine them.

Questions to assess language development

EXPRESSIVE LANGUAGE

Can children label items as they note them on the walk?

Can children use a descriptor to tell something about the items they find?

RECEPTIVE LANGUAGE

Can children locate various items as they are named?

Literacy Connections

• •

Nature Walk by Douglas Florian

A mother and her two children go on a nature walk through the woods.

The Perfect Spot by Robert J. Blake

Dad is looking for just the right spot to paint, and his curious young son wants a spot to catch frogs and such. Only after Dad unwinds a bit with the boy does he notice the beauty of nature all around.

What Joe Saw by Anna Grossnickle Hines

Joe lags behind the rest of his class as they race to the park. Joe's slower pace allows him to observe all kinds of natural wonders.

WRITING EXPERIENCES
• •

● Invite children to take clipboards with them on their walk. Encourage children to make observational drawings of things they see, hear, or feel on their walk. Invite them to write or dictate captions for their drawings.

● Encourage children to write or dictate letters home to families describing what they experienced on their walk.

● Help children sort their observations by making various charts to record what they saw or experienced. For example, one chart could be labeled "Animals We Saw." Another could be "Flowers We Found" or "Trash Around Our Center." Children can tell what they saw while you write their words on the chart.

Art

DOUBLE EASEL

CRAYONS

PAINT BRUSH

MARKERS

PLAYDOUGH

SCISSORS

Tell Me About Your Picture

Children enjoy showing others their drawings. This interchange provides an excellent opportunity for the use of descriptive language as the children talk about their creations. An adult who shows interest and is willing to listen is in for a treat.

What you will need

Paint and paintbrushes, crayons, or markers

Paper

Words you can use

tell

good

colors

about

like

big

share

more

little

paint

crayon

draw

endless descriptors depending on topic of drawing

What to do

● Give the children numerous opportunities throughout the day to draw, paint, or color pictures of recent happenings in their lives, characters from a story they have heard, or anything else that interests them.

● Ask the children to tell about their pictures in a small group setting or when alone with you. Listen carefully as they use language to describe the picture and the story that it tells. Most children will do this willingly if they have an active listener. That is the critical component of this activity. If you ask, then actively listen with genuine interest. Ask open-ended questions to encourage the child to elaborate.

More

Using the same listening skills, allow the children numerous opportunities to describe what they have done, be it block building, a sandcastle, a game they have played, or anything that they perceive as an accomplishment.

Questions to assess language development

EXPRESSIVE LANGUAGE

Are the children combining words as they describe their creations—noun + verb, adjective + noun?

Can children formulate answers to different types of questions?

Can children respond to questions in a sequential order—first, I drew a _____, then I drew the _____?

Are the children using age-appropriate vocabulary and specific words to describe their creations? Do they describe shape, size, color, and other advanced concepts?

Remember to pose open-ended questions for the children to answer. These should be questions that begin with two key words: *How* or *Why*.

Open-ended questions should encourage elaboration.

Open-ended questions should not be answerable with *Yes* or *No*.

Literacy Connections

READING EXPERIENCES

Cool Ali by Nancy Poydar

During the heat of the summer, Ali draws cool chalk pictures on the sidewalk. All her neighbors gather around the pictures of lakes and snow to cool off.

Emma's Rug by Allen Say

Young Emma uses her special rug for inspiration for her wonderful drawings. When her rug gets washed, Emma thinks she can't draw, but realizes her ideas are all around her.

The Fantastic Drawings of Danielle by Barbara McClintock

Danielle tries to draw realistic pictures like her father's photographs, but they always turn out as fantasy drawings. Finally her fanciful creatures bring her good fortune.

WRITING EXPERIENCES

- Write down the children's words as they describe their pictures. Read the captions back to the children. Display the children's art and captions, referring to them regularly. Point to the words as you read.

- If appropriate, have the children write their own captions in rough draft form. Then rewrite the captions in standard spelling before displaying them or publishing them in books.

Art Show

This creative activity lets children work, cooperate, and talk together.

What you will need

Sidewalk chalk of varying colors
Blue ribbons

Words you can use

draw
art
show
together
color names
ribbons
sidewalk
walk
chalk
picture

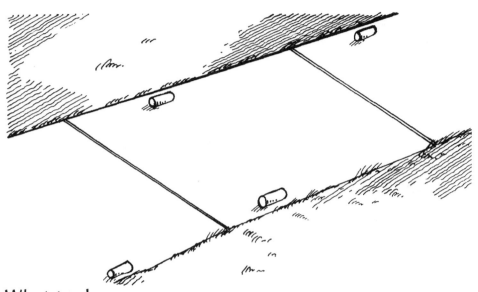

What to do

- Talk with the children about what an art show is.
- If the children would like to have an art show, begin by taking a small group outside.
- Divide the children into pairs and give each child a piece of colored sidewalk chalk.
- Ask each pair to draw a picture together on the sidewalk, using both colors of chalk.
- The children complete their pictures, working and talking together.
- Take a walk, observing each group's creation.
- Award each picture a "blue ribbon."
- On another day try this with teams of three or more children.

Questions to assess language development

EXPRESSIVE LANGUAGE

Are children using the politeness markers such as *please* and *thank you* as they attempt to work as a team?

What kinds of art vocabulary are being generated?

RECEPTIVE LANGUAGE

Are both children in each pair taking the roles of initiator and responder, showing both expressive and receptive language skills?

Literacy Connections

READING EXPERIENCES

Art Dog by Thacher Hurd

> This funny book tells how Art Dog rescues valuable masterpieces that were stolen from the Dogopolis Museum of art.

The Paper Princess by Elisa Kleven

> A little girl's drawing of a princess is blown away by the wind before she can finish it. Landing in the beak of a blue jay, the picture is finished and returned to the girl.

Regina's Big Mistake by Marissa Moss

> Regina, unsure of her artistic talent, copies another kid's pictures. When she makes a mistake, she turns her dented sun into a moon, building her confidence as an artist.

WRITING EXPERIENCES

- Turn the art center into an art museum by creating special places for displaying children's artwork. Invite children to label and caption their pieces before displaying them.

- Invite children to make signs for their museum. Signs might include the name of the museum, hours of operation, rules, and special sections such as paintings, sculptures, etc.

- Provide writing materials for children to write positive comments about other children's artwork. For example, help children write what they like about a particular piece.

Color Creations

By exploring and mixing familiar colors the children learn that they can create new colors. Language targets include new vocabulary and emerging literacy skills.

What you will need

Fingerpaint (red, yellow, blue)

Paper

Teaspoons

Book about color mixing (see suggestions below)

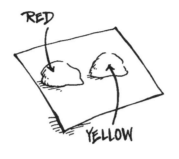

Words you can use

color	red
purple	yellow
green	orange
blue	
made	
make	
picture	
create	
feel	
mix	
fingers	
touch	
find	
move	
squishy	
two	
one	
discover	
new	
together	
happening	
predict	

What to do

- Place one teaspoon of red and one teaspoon of yellow fingerpaint on each child's paper.
- Ask the children to identify the two colors of fingerpaint on their paper. Help them identify if necessary.
- Tell the children to mix the two colors together with their fingers.
- As they mix the colors ask them to notice what is happening. Are the colors still the same? What color have they made?
- Mix some other colors and see if they can make and identify new colors, using new paper for each mixture.
- Ask them to predict what color they think they'll get. The children can mix red and blue for purple, blue and yellow for green.
- After the children have made their own discoveries read *White Rabbit's Color Book* (or any other book listed on the next page), an excellent story about a white rabbit that makes similar color mixture discoveries as he climbs in and out of paint cans.

More

Experiment mixing colors of playdough, tempera paints, and crayons.

Literacy Connections

READING EXPERIENCES

Color by Ruth Heller
> Written in rhyme, this book deals with the concept of color and what happens when colors are combined.

Little Blue and Little Yellow by Leo Lionni
> When little dots of blue and yellow hug, they become green, making it impossible for their parents to recognize them.

Mouse Paint by Ellen Stoll Walsh
> Three white mice climb into jars of paint and make new colors as they step in each other's puddles.

White Rabbit's Color Book by Alan Baker
> A white rabbit makes discoveries about new colors as he climbs in and out of paint cans.

● After reading a book such as *Mouse Paint* or *White Rabbit's Color Book*, help children retell the story by using a clothesline story. Stretch a string between two tables. Using clothespins, pin photocopies or drawings of some of the illustrations from the book in order on the string. Have children tell the story while pointing to or walking from illustration to illustration.

WRITING EXPERIENCES

● Help children make a class book by stapling together the papers on which they created new colors. On each page, write how the child created the new color. For example, "Sara made green with blue and yellow." Read the class book together, and then put it in the class library for children to read alone and to each other.

● Have children talk about how they made new colors. Write down their words on a large piece of paper. Read this chart with the children.

● Have small blank books available with the following title, "My Color Book." Allow children to write and draw using crayons or markers. You may want to write their words for them. Encourage children to take their books home to read to their families.

Questions to assess language development

EXPRESSIVE LANGUAGE

Can the children say the names of the primary colors?

Can the children say the names of the secondary colors?

RECEPTIVE LANGUAGE

Do the children know the names of the primary colors?

Do the children know the names of the secondary colors?

All Bark No Bites

Bark is the skin of a tree. It protects and helps to nourish the tree. Children can use descriptive language as they describe the texture and appearance of the bark.

What you will need

Paper

Crayons

Wooded area with mature and aging trees

Collecting bags

Words you can use

collect	bark
tree	woods
rubbings	crayons
texture	feel
touch	old
dead	living
skin	pull
thick	thin
rough	smooth
curved	straight
bumpy	wet
dry	rot

BARK

RUBBING

What to do

● Take a walk in a wooded area.

● Collect the loose bark from the ground and place in plastic collecting bags.

● As the children collect the bark, ask them how it feels as they touch it.

● Take this collecting opportunity to talk about the care of trees and how important the bark is to the trees' good health. Point out that disease and insects can get into the tree if the bark is damaged, so it is important that bark is not pulled off living trees.

● Upon return to the center, examine the bark collections and talk about the children's perceptions of bark textures.

● Sort the bark collections into different categories, such as smooth, rough, bumpy, thick, thin, curved, flat.

● Make crayon rubbings of the bark and let the children use inventive spelling to write about the texture on their rubbing.

Questions to assess language development

Do children use a variety of the above words to describe the bark?

Can you model various terms to increase the use by the children?

Literacy Connections

READING EXPERIENCES

A B Cedar: An Alphabet of Trees by George Ella Lyon

> Each alphabet letter is illustrated with leaf and fruit samples of a tree and a silhouette drawing of the tree.

A Tree Is Nice by Janice May Udry

> This book gives reasons why a tree is nice.

Red Leaf, Yellow Leaf by Lois Ehlert

> This book tells the story of a sugar maple seed that takes root in the forest.

WRITING EXPERIENCES

● Help children staple the pages of their crayon rubbings to make their own books. They can read their books to each other, and then take them home to read to their families.

● Make an experience chart of the walk. Let children retell what they did, and write what they say on a large piece of paper. Read their story back to them, read it together, and encourage them to read to themselves and each other.

● Have blank books available with the following titles: "Smooth," "Rough," "Bumpy," and so on. Encourage children to draw and write about things that would fit in each book.

Color Rubbings

The environment of the early childhood center provides a rich resource of textures to touch and feel. Both receptive and expressive language skills are developed as the children create color rubbings.

What you will need

White paper
Crayons

Words you can use

rubbing
texture
find
feel
hard
soft
rough
smooth
bumpy
outdoors
trees
bark
leaves
grass
twigs
sticks
rocks
wall
sidewalk
fence
press
hard
color names

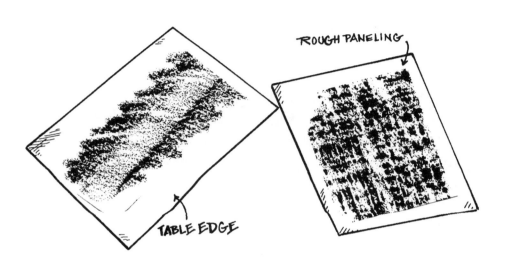

ROUGH PANELING

TABLE EDGE

What to do

● Give each child a piece of white paper and a rubbing crayon.
● Let the children explore and do crayon rubbings of the various textures that they find in the classroom, such as the rug, table, chair, floor, door.
● If desired, go outdoors. Nature texture rubbings such as tree bark, leaves, grass, twigs, and rocks are abundant. The school grounds can also provide rubbing opportunities, such as a wall, sidewalk, playground equipment, and fences.
● Ask the children how the rubbing surfaces feel. Are they hard, soft, rough, smooth, bumpy, and so on?
● Display the rubbings.

More

Make rubbings on small pieces of white cotton sheets, about four inches by four inches (ten centimeters by ten centimeters). Frame and send home as a gift from the child to the family.

Make a class quilt by sewing the separate rubbings together. Display the quilt in the classroom.

Questions to assess language development

EXPRESSIVE LANGUAGE

Can the children name a variety of colors?

Can the children name the environmental items they are using for their rubbings?

Can the children name descriptors of the various textures they are producing?

RECEPTIVE LANGUAGE

Are the children able to "show" and "talk about" their various productions, showing both receptive and expressive language?

Literacy Connections

READING EXPERIENCES

The Color Box by Dayle Ann Dodds

A monkey finds a box that's all black inside, except for a dot of yellow. He climbs through to find everything there is yellow. The next spot he climbs through leads him to the color found in the illustration on the next page. The rhyming story covers eight colors.

Color Dance by Ann Jonas

Three children dance with red, blue, and yellow scarves to show how colors are made by overlaying them.

Lunch by Denise Fleming

The hungry gray mouse fills up on colorful fruits and vegetables. Bright illustrations allow readers to predict what he will eat next.

WRITING EXPERIENCES

- Invite children to make books of their rubbings. Staple their rubbings together and help them write or take dictation describing the item.
- Children can make rubbing riddles. Have them display each rubbing with a clue about what made the rubbing. On the back or on a separate sheet, they can draw and label the answer.

Make a Shape

The ability to match, sort, and identify shapes is a cognitive prerequisite for young children. Children will enjoy making shapes and talking about them.

What you will need

Playdough or clay
Shape cutters
Rolling pins

Words you can use

roll
press
dough
clay
square
star
circle
oval/egg
diamond
rectangle
triangle
shape
next
rolling pin
cutters

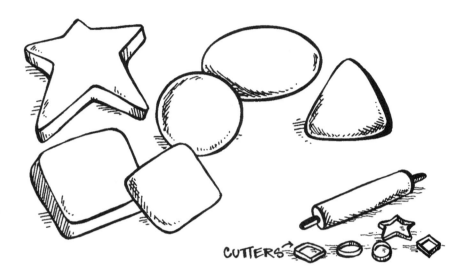

CUTTERS

What to do

- Give a small group of children clay or dough and cutters in various shapes.
- The children roll the dough, then cut out shapes using the cutters.
- Encourage the children to name the shapes as they cut them out.
- Talk about sorting the shapes into groups, such as by shape, color, clay vs. dough, etc.

More

Develop patterns by sequencing shapes into rows.

Questions to assess language development

EXPRESSIVE LANGUAGE

Can children name the basic shapes of circle, square, triangle, and rectangle?

Can children say *why* they have put certain shapes into certain groups? For example, color, all circles, all made of clay, etc.

RECEPTIVE LANGUAGE

Can the children identify various shapes?

Can children sort according to some similarities within the shapes they have created?

Literacy Connections

READING EXPERIENCES

Grandfather Tang's Story by Ann Tompert

Grandfather Tang uses tangrams to show each character as he tells his granddaughter a story. Illustrations include a black tangram diagram that shows how to arrange the tangrams into each animal.

Sea Shapes by Suse MacDonald

In three-panel illustrations, simple shapes transform into ocean animals.

The Secret Birthday Message by Eric Carle

Tim must follow the secret messages written in rebus clues to find his birthday present—a new puppy. The colorful illustrations include cutouts that correspond to the shape clues.

WRITING EXPERIENCES

● Have available a variety of blank books cut into shapes. Children can draw, write, or dictate about things that are the same shape as the book.

● Invite children on a Shape Hunt. Give children a clipboard or a piece of heavy cardboard with a spring clip on top to hold paper. As they walk around the room, building, play yard, and other area, they draw, write, or dictate the names of things they see that are a certain shape. Lists can be shared and discussed.

● Have available a variety of shapes pre-cut from construction paper. Invite children to paste the shapes down into a figure. Encourage them to talk about their figure, then write or dictate a caption. Display captioned shape figures, reading the captions and encouraging children to read their captions to others.

Sound Pictures

Sounds are part of memories. This activity reinforces listening skills as well as a logical thinking as children categorize things that go together.

What you will need

Crayons
Drawing paper

Words you can use

listen
hear
make
names of environmental sounds

What to do

- Talk with the children about environmental sounds that they might be familiar with, such as a car starting, bird singing, or ball bouncing.
- Tell them that they hear sounds when they listen with their ears. Ask them to tell about some of the sounds that they hear when they go outside.
- Ask them to make a picture of something that they like to hear.
- Let the children share the sound pictures they have made. Ask them to tell you what makes that sound and why they like it.
- Encourage them to categorize the sounds that they think go together.

More

Ask the children to draw animals that make sounds they enjoy, as well as things from the city, country, school, and home that make interesting sounds.

Questions to assess language development

Can the children name sources of sounds, with pictures and without the picture cues?

RECEPTIVE LANGUAGE

Can the children tell one sound from another? (This ability is called auditory discrimination.)

Literacy Connections

READING EXPERIENCES

Early Morning in the Barn by Nancy Tafuri

> The barn comes alive with the sounds of waking animals.

Pots and Pans by Patricia Hubbell

> This book celebrates the noisy fun of a toddler's first exploration in the pantry.

Splash, Splash by Jeff Sheppard

> Clumsy animals fall into the water with a splash and predictable noise.

WRITING EXPERIENCES

- Encourage children to write or dictate a caption for their pictures.
- Class books or individual books can be made with titles such as "Loud Noises," "Quiet Noises," "Animal Noises," and so on. Children can draw and write or dictate about things that make these noises.
- Encourage children to write down things they hear in different places: the classroom, cafeteria, hall, playground, and so on. Their individual lists can be combined into class charts.

Places We Go

Children can use their imaginations to travel to many places. They also travel to places in their real world. Sharing these travels, near and far, is an excellent opportunity to develop and practice descriptive words.

What you will need

Drawing paper

Crayons, markers, or paint and paintbrushes

Words you can use

place

travel

went

go

transportation

names of places—church, grocery store, the mall, shoe store, restaurant, drug store, doctor's office, hospital, dentist's office, grandparents' home, hardware store, book store

GRANDPARENTS   BOOK STORE

What to do

● Following a long weekend or a vacation break, ask the children to make a drawing of a place they visited.

● Each child describes his drawing as he talks about his weekend or vacation destinations. Remember these excursions do not have to be trips to exotic places.

More

Ask the children to describe what they did at their destination.

Questions to assess language development

EXPRESSIVE LANGUAGE

Are the children participating in discussions about their drawings?

RECEPTIVE LANGUAGE

What kinds of prompts are needed to engage the children?

Literacy Connections

Emma's Vacation by David McPhail

Although Emma's parents take her to all the exciting vacation spots, she would prefer the outdoor life of wading, fishing, and eating berries.

The Journey Home by Alison Lester

A brother and sister dig in their sand pit and fall through to the North Pole. On their trip home they meet up with Santa, the Good Fairy, the Little Mermaid, and others.

Love, Your Bear Pete by Dyan Sheldon

Brenda leaves her bear on the bus and begins receiving postcards from him from all around the world.

WRITING EXPERIENCES

- Have children write or dictate captions for their drawings.
- After a field trip, encourage children to draw and write postcards describing their adventure.
- Invite children to keep journals of important things they do each day. They can write or dictate about things that happen at school or home.

How Did You Go?

Getting there is as much fun as the destination. In this activity, children use travel words to describe ways in which they've travelled.

What you will need

Paper

Crayons, markers, or paints and
    paintbrushes

Words you can use

travel

car

truck

airplane

jet

train

boat

wagon

tricycle

motorcycle

scooter

transportation

place

destination

ferry

tram

streetcar

bus

What to do

- Ask the children to share the types of transportation they use to travel from home to school.
- Ask them what other forms of transportation they use to get from place to place.
- Ask them to make a picture of the kind of transportation they use the most and the kind of transportation their parents use the most.
- Talk about the types of transportation that are present at school, such as a tricycle, wagon, and scooter.
- Talk about and compare the types of transportation that children and adults use.

More

Talk about modes of transportation that do not have wheels.

Make a map listing the places the children travel to—town, city, state, nation, world.

Questions to assess language development

Can the children provide names (labels) for the various transportation items?

Are they expanding their concept of transportation by naming and identifying new forms of transportation that they may not have tried, but understand are "ways to go places?"

RECEPTIVE LANGUAGE

Are the children familiar with a variety of ways to go?

Literacy Connections

READING EXPERIENCES

Dinosaurs Travel by Laura K. Brown and Marc Brown

> This book follows a family of dinosaurs on their travels and describes such modes of transportation as the skateboard, bike, car, subway, bus, train, boat, and airplane.

The Wheels on the Bus by Maryann Kovalski

> Grandma and the children sing this familiar song while they wait for the bus. They get so involved that they miss the bus and have to take a taxi.

This is the Way We Go to School: A Book About Children Around the World by Edith Baer

> Written in rhyming couplets, this book tells of children around the world going to school in a variety of ways: on foot and bicycle, in ferries and cable cars, and by boats and skis.

● Create a word wall of transportation words. On large cards write names of vehicles or other transportation-related vocabulary. Tape cards to the wall. Point to and read the words regularly. Encourage children to read the words on their own.

WRITING EXPERIENCES

● Encourage children to record how they came to school. This can be done on a chart, graph, class book, or wall display.

● Using large pictures of various modes of transportation, take children's dictation about the picture. Record their words under or around the picture. Read the chart together and refer to it regularly for several days.

Snowman

The construction of a paper snowman can target size concepts as well as position words. The creativity expressed in the adding of individual parts can also spark conversation among the children.

What you will need

Construction paper—one dark sheet per child

White construction paper circles in various sizes

Assorted paper

Scissors

Yarn, or fabric for noses, buttons, hats, etc.

Glue

Words you can use

big

bigger

biggest

small

smaller

smallest

on top of

on the bottom

middle-sized

in the middle

under

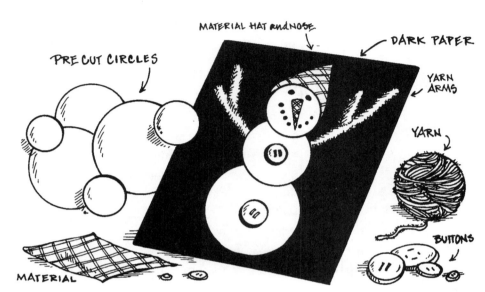

What to do

- Offer children in the art center various-sized white circles. (Older children can cut out their own.) Also give the children a dark sheet of construction paper for a background.

- Ask the children to show and name any big circles, any small circles, and/or any middle-sized circles that they might have chosen. The children can glue the circles onto their dark background paper to make their snowman.

- As they complete their snowmen, ask the children about the circles at the top, at the bottom, or in the middle of their snowman.

- If desired, the children add individual noses, hats, buttons, and other decorations.

More

Introduce comparative and superlative words, such as *bigger, biggest, smaller, smallest.*

Use words such as *same* and *different.*

Create an extended "snow family."

Questions to assess language development

RECEPTIVE LANGUAGE

Are the children familiar with the polar opposites *big* and *little*?

Can they identify top, bottom, and in the middle?

Are they familiar with the concept of snowmen?

Literacy Connections

READING EXPERIENCES

Snow Magic by Harriet Ziefert

> All of the snow people are getting together for a snow party because it's the first snow of the year on the first day of winter.

Snowballs by Lois Ehlert

> Each of the snow creatures photographed in this book is finished with a wide variety of real objects. At the end of the book, the objects are pictured and labeled.

Snowy Day by Ezra Jack Keats

> This is a simple story of a young boy's delight during his first snowfall.

WRITING EXPERIENCES

- Invite children to write or dictate captions describing their finished snow people.

- On a large piece of chart paper, write the children's words as they tell how to make a snowman step by step.

- Staple some of the cut-out circles into blank books. Have these available for children to write their own stories about snowmen.

Winter Play

This activity encourages children to explore nature and language terms pertaining to winter.

What you will need

Scissors
Paper
Glue
String
Plexiglas
Warm clothing

Words you can use

snow
ice
snowstorm
freezing
quiet
sleet
rain
winter
icicles
cold
snowflakes
different
fall
wet
snow angels
snowmen

What to do

- On a day when snow is forecast, make snowflakes out of paper. They can be very simple designs, with a few cuts, or as elaborate as the children want to make them.

- Discuss how each snowflake is different, like the children themselves. No two snowflakes look alike.

- Each child can glue his snowflake on one large piece of colored paper, or hang them from the ceiling on pieces of string so they can dangle.

- Take the children outside when it is snowing. Use a flat piece of Plexiglas to catch snowflakes as they fall. Encourage the children to look at the snowflakes, noticing the detail, the size, and how they are all different.

- Explore other snow or ice formations. Look at hanging icicles and snow drifts. Encourage children to pick up snow and describe how it feels. Have them pack it tight, roll it in snowballs, then break the snowballs.

- Describe how the snow is falling. Note how quiet it is.

- Play in the snow. Let the children initiate the play; if needed, offer suggestions to make snow angels, snowmen, snow houses, and igloos.

More

Talk about sleet, ice, rain.

Talk about Native Americans (Inuit) and animals that live primarily in cold places.

Questions to assess language development

EXPRESSIVE LANGUAGE

Do the children note the differences in the snowflakes? Are they able to verbalize the differences?

RECEPTIVE LANGUAGE

Does the general seasonal concept of winter come to life for the children?

Literacy Connections

READING EXPERIENCES

Ice Cream Bear by Jez Alborough
One day, just when Bear runs out of ice cream, it begins to snow ice cream. He makes a giant ball of it, providing a dream come true—or is it?

It's Snowing! It's Snowing! by Jack Prelutsky
This book contains 17 poems about fun in the snow.

Katy and the Big Snow by Virginia Lee Burton
The classic story of Katy the tractor plowing the town out from under a giant snow fall.

Snow on Snow on Snow by Cheryl Chapman
A young child puts on "clothes over clothes over clothes" before going out for a sled ride with his dog.

WRITING EXPERIENCES

- Record the children's play in the snow on an experience chart. Invite the children to tell about what they did in the snow. Write their words on a large piece of chart paper. Read the account back to the children, pointing to the words. Encourage the children to read along. Leave the chart out for the children to refer to.

- Have small blank books available for children to draw, write, or dictate their personal stories about playing in the snow.

Topic Collages

Cooperation, sharing, and conversation are three essential elements in this activity. The children will also create a product that can be used in the classroom.

What you will need

Poster board

Glue

Scissors

Old magazines, newspapers, cards

Words you can use

group

toy words

clothing words

animal names

politeness markers (yes, no, please, pass the _____)

What to do

● Divide the children into a few large or small groups, depending on the needs and abilities of the children in the class.

● Give each group one large piece of poster board; scissors; glue; and magazines, papers, or cards to cut up.

● Ask the children to find pictures from one topic, group, or category and to cut those pictures out. Suggested topics should reflect the interests of the children. These might include animals, toys, clothing, homes, and families.

● The children glue their pictures onto the appropriate poster board by topic.

● If a child knows an item that belongs on a particular topic collage and can't find a picture, he could draw that item onto the collage.

● Encourage the children to name the items in the collage. Help them if needed.

● Display these topic collages and use them for conversation starters or as displays for parent visits. If they are displayed, encourage the children to add additional items to the collages.

Questions to assess language development

EXPRESSIVE LANGUAGE

Are the children able to name a variety of items in each category?

Can they work collaboratively, using appropriate social language?

RECEPTIVE LANGUAGE

Can they find pictures or illustrate those items into the appropriate category?

Literacy Connections

READING EXPERIENCES

My First Riddles by Judith Hoffman Corwin

> This book of riddles is illustrated with spectacular fabric collages that offer a variety of visual clues.

The Paper Dragon by Marguerite W. Davol

> A Chinese legend about courage and wisdom beautifully illustrated with fold-out pages of Chinese art.

Rooster's Off to See the World by Eric Carle

> All the pictures in this enjoyable book are collages.

WRITING EXPERIENCES

- Help children write captions for their collages. They can write or dictate words and sentences to describe their art.
- Use completed collages as book covers. Children can write about and illustrate the topic depicted in their collage.
- Cut postcard-size pieces from finished collages. Let the children use these postcards to write to friends and family members about their activities.

Popsicle Puppets

The children create their own popsicle puppet characters, then recreate a known story or make up one of their own. This activity stresses narrative development, sequencing, cooperation, and use of dialogue.

What you will need

Popsicle sticks
Glue
Yarn
Scissors
Construction paper
Crayons
Fabric
Storybook

Words you can use

pretend
story
beginning
middle
end
puppet
act out
tell

THE 3 LITTLE PIGS

THE BIG BAD WOLF

What to do

● Provide art materials, including crayons, construction paper, scissors, glue, and popsicle sticks.

● Ask the children what kind of puppets they would like to make to depict a familiar children's story, such as "The Three Bears" and "The Three Little Pigs."

● Make the puppets for the story, assisting as needed. (See illustration for directions.)

● The children act out the story from behind a table or desk with their popsicle puppets.

More

Depending on the abilities of the children, encourage them to act out a more complicated story, or use a less structured plot to allow children to be more creative.

Use additional art materials to enhance the puppets, such as yarn, buttons, fabric, etc.

Questions to assess language development

EXPRESSIVE LANGUAGE

Can they manipulate the puppets as characters?

Are the children more interested in the stories they make up than in set narratives?

RECEPTIVE LANGUAGE

Are children familiar with stories from selections of children's literature?

Are they able to follow a story line?

Literacy Connections

READING EXPERIENCES

Onstage and Backstage at the Night Owl Theatre by Ann Hayes

A cast of animal characters works hard to put on the play "Cinderella." This book offers lots of "theatre" words.

The Three Billy Goats Gruff illustrated by Stephen Carpenter

Great for acting out with puppets, this classic story tells about three billy goats that outwit a clumsy troll.

● To help children develop a sense of story, occasionally create a story map after reading. On a piece of chart paper, write down important elements from the story, such as characters and events.

WRITING EXPERIENCES

● Invite children to draw and write about the stories they hear and read. Story journals allow children to respond to how they feel about stories and how they relate to the characters and situations. Model how to write responses.

● Children can keep reading logs of books they have heard or read. Each child can keep an individual log of his own readings. The class can keep a list of all the books read aloud.

Emotion Puppets

This activity encourages children to think and verbalize about specific times or occasions, such as birthdays and bedtimes.

What you will need

Tongue depressors

Yarn

Glue

Pencils and crayons

2 construction paper circles per
   child

Words you can use

happy

sad

glad

unhappy

mad

eyes

nose

mouth

hair

chin

eyebrows

eyelashes

cheeks

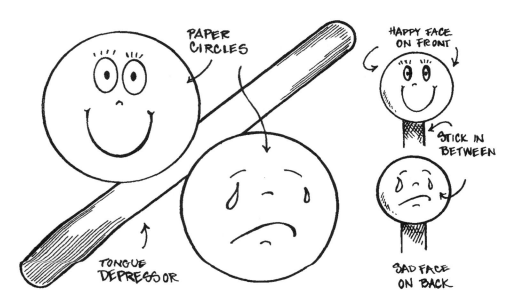

What to do

- Give each child one tongue depressor, two circles of construction paper (faces), yarn, pencils, crayons, and glue.
- Invite the children to draw a "happy" face on one of their circles, and a "sad" face on the other circle. Depending on the abilities of the children, make faces representing a wider scope of emotions.
- The children glue a face on each side of the tongue depressor with the picture of the face out. (See illustration.)
- The children continue to finish their faces with hair and additional facial features as they choose.
- When the puppets are complete, ask the children to show their "happy" face puppet. Then ask the children to show their "sad" face puppet.
- If appropriate, ask the children why their puppets feel a certain way. Or ask children to show the puppet that tells how they feel when they open a present, or fall and hurt their knee, or see a new puppy.

Questions to assess language development

EXPRESSIVE LANGUAGE

Are the children able to put these emotion words into context?

Can the children use words beyond the basic happy/sad emotions to express the puppet's "feelings?"

RECEPTIVE LANGUAGE

Are the children understanding the basic polar opposites of happy/sad?

Literacy Connections

READING EXPERIENCES

Feelings by Aliki

> The author presents children showing a variety of feelings in different situations. Short vignettes are shared through interesting illustrations and text.

How Do I Feel? by Norma Simon

> Carl shares events in his life concerning his twin brother and his grandparents. He asks, "How do I feel?" then answers his own question by describing his feelings.

Mean Soup by Betsy Everitt

> When Horace comes home from school in a bad mood, Mom helps him shout and stir away his angry feelings into a special broth that cooks up good feelings.

My Many Colored Days by Dr. Seuss

> "Some days are yellow. Some are blue. On different days I'm different too." The rhyming story goes on to describe how different feelings are all part of being who we are.

WRITING EXPERIENCES

- Children can contribute individual pages to a series of class books about feelings. For example, they can add pages to books titled "That Makes Me Mad," "That Makes Me Laugh," "That Makes Me Sad," and so on. Children can illustrate and write or dictate about things and situations that cause those feelings.

- Encourage children to write messages to people to share their feelings with them; for example, "I felt happy when you _____."

- Create a class chart by recording children's words as they explain what they do when they're sad or mad or happy.

A Special Card for You

Making greeting cards to celebrate special family days reinforces emerging literacy skills, learning color names, and discussion skills.

What you will need

Scissors

Construction paper (primary colors)

Crayons, pencils

Picture magazines or precut pictures

Glue, paste, tape

Words you can use

card

message

celebrate

greeting

decorate

draw

cut

scissors

tear

decorate

favorite

like

magazine

picture

activity

collage

holiday

family names

primary color names

birthday, other special family days

What to do

- If possible, have the children choose a piece of construction paper by naming the color that they want to make the greeting card.
- Fold the paper in half. The greeting (such as for a birthday or Mother's Day) will be placed on the inside fold.
- The children can decorate the cover with precut pictures or with pictures they cut from magazines.
- Ask the children what they feel the card recipient likes to do.
- Have the children go through magazines tearing or cutting out pictures that show items or activities that the family member enjoys.
- The children paste the pictures on the card cover, making a collage of the things the family member likes.
- Have each child dictate a special greeting to the card recipient. For example, ask, "What message would you like to send to Mother?" Write this message in the card.
- The child can sign the card and deliver it personally or mail it.

More

The children can draw or color a favorite activity for the card cover.

Questions to assess language development

Can children respond to *Who* questions?

Can children respond to *What* questions?

RECEPTIVE LANGUAGE

Can children respond to directions to construct the card?

Literacy Connections

READING EXPERIENCES

Birthdays! Celebrating Life Around the World by Eve B. Feldman

> Using children's artwork and simple text, this book takes the readers on a special trip to find out how birthdays are observed around the world.

Don't Forget to Write by Marina Selway

> When Rosie goes to stay on the farm with Granddad and Aunty Mabel, she writes a long letter home, telling her mother how every day is a special day.

WRITING EXPERIENCES

- On a calendar, help children write their names and birthdays.

- Encourage children to write or dictate cards and letters for friends and family members.

- Make a class book about birthdays. Encourage each child to illustrate or bring a photo of something they did on their last birthday. Let them write or dictate about their picture. Fasten pages into a book. After reading the completed book together, put the book in the class library.

The Wheels Go Around

By using wheels from broken toys, the children can create individual art prints. Descriptive words to describe the size, shape, and origin of the wheels could evolve with this activity.

What you will need

Paper

Wheels from discarded toys

Tempera paint

Containers for paint

Words you can use

wheels	round
print	picture
art	paint
toy	around
dip	color names

Questions to assess language development

EXPRESSIVE LANGUAGE

Can the children name various sources for the wheels?

RECEPTIVE LANGUAGE

Can the children identify which wheels appear to be the same or different?

What to do

- As small wheel toys break, collect the wheels. Also ask families to collect wheels and send them to school.
- Place the collection of wheels in the art center.
- The children dip the wheels into tempera paint and make various print patterns on paper.
- A discussion of types of wheels, sizes, shapes, and origin will evolve as the children make their wheel prints.

Literacy Connections

READING EXPERIENCES

How Many Trucks Can a Tow Truck Tow? By Charlotte Pomerantz

A little truck becomes a hero in this story told in rhyme, with brightly colored illustrations of tow trucks.

My Bike by Donna Jakob

Yesterday the pedals got stuck, the front wheel wobbled, and there was lots of falling. Today, bike riding is filled with success.

Train Song by Diane Siebert

Clickety-clack, clickety-clack go the wheels of the moving train in this beautifully illustrated picture book.

WRITING EXPERIENCES

- Using pictures of different kinds of wheels, take children's dictation about wheels. Encourage children to describe the wheels and how they are used while you write down their words on chart paper.
- Have small blank books available for children to illustrate different vehicles with wheels. Encourage them to write words to describe the vehicles, or write their words for them in their books.

Sand and Water

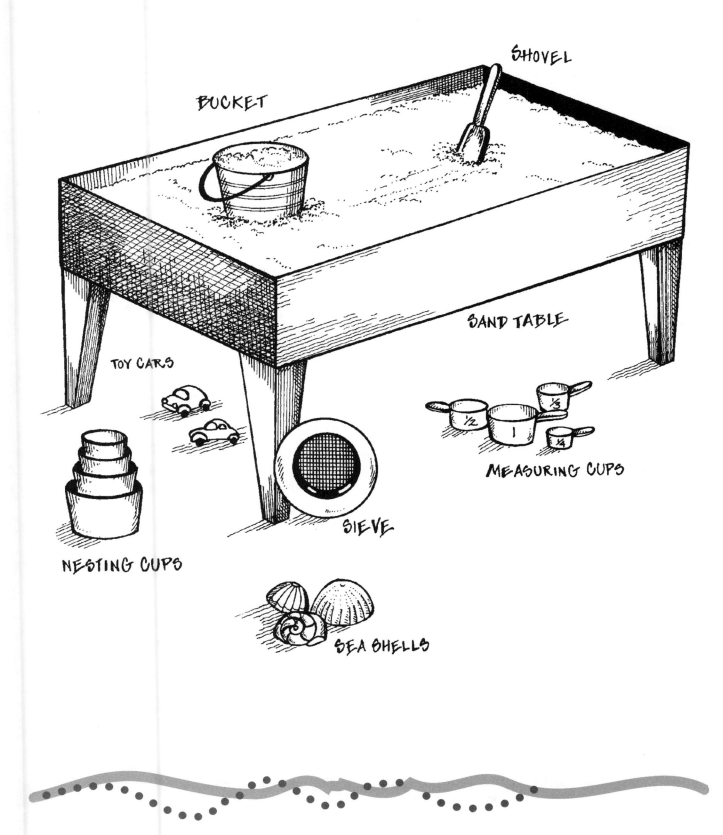

BUCKET

SHOVEL

SAND TABLE

TOY CARS

NESTING CUPS

SIEVE

SEA SHELLS

MEASURING CUPS

½ 1 ⅓ ¼

Color Fish

The ability to match, identify, and label colors is an important pre-academic skill for young children. This fun activity teaches color naming skills through play, so that both receptive and expressive language abilities are practiced.

What you will need

Sand/water table
Water
Plastic fish
Small aquarium nets

Words you can use

catch
swim
caught
fish
water
net
swam
ocean
sea
river
lake
color words

What to do

● Fill the water table with water and plastic fish in the three primary colors.

● Give the children small fishing nets (the type that are used with aquariums).

● Encourage them to "fish" with the nets and catch the fish from the water. Children may fish for only one color, or name the color fish they caught and then sort them into matching groups.

More

A broader color base can be used, incorporating various colors at a developmentally appropriate level.

Other plastic animals in specific colors can be used.

Questions to assess language development

EXPRESSIVE LANGUAGE

Can the children name the color of the fish they catch?

RECEPTIVE LANGUAGE

Can the children catch fish of a certain color when named by the teacher?

Can the children sort fish groups by color?

Literacy Connections

READING EXPERIENCES

A Color of His Own by Leo Lionni

A chameleon wants a color of his own like all the other animals, instead of always changing colors to match his surroundings.

Fish Is Fish by Leo Lionni

When Minnow's friend Frog tells him about the exciting life on land, Minnow tries it out, only to find himself gasping for air. Frog comes to the rescue and convinces his friend that fish is fish.

The Rainbow Fish by Marcus Pfister

A beautiful fish with sparkling scales finds that beauty doesn't guarantee friends. When he shares his scales with others, he finds that giving is a good thing.

WRITING EXPERIENCES

● Have available small blank books with pages of colored paper. Invite the children to illustrate items of specific colors and to write about each colored item.

● Encourage the children to draw and write using only a specified color.

● Make a class chart of things the children find that are of a specified color. Use that color to write on the chart.

Bubble Talk

Bubbles are fascinating for children of all ages, with their interesting spherical shapes, fragile nature, and beautiful colors. Children can verbalize one word commands such as *blow* and *pop* in this activity as well as describe the bubbles and their floating actions.

What you will need

Liquid soap (Dawn)

Glycerin

Water

Measuring cup

Teaspoon

2-liter soda bottle

Cake pans

Bubble blowers

Words you can use

bubbles	blow
breath	fly
up	down
float	watch
see	wet
air	blower
create	make
messy	measure
mix	mixture
recipe	color words
shape words	beautiful
pop	

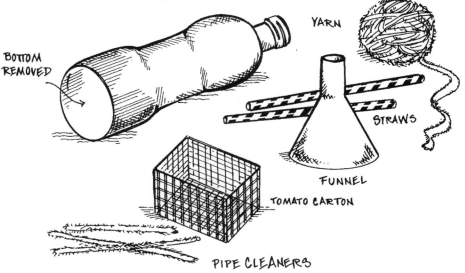

What to do

- Let the children mix the bubble solution (see recipe below).
- Pour the completed bubble solution into a cake pan.
- Provide a variety of bubble blowers such as funnels; plastic soda bottles with bottoms removed; pipe cleaners that can be shaped by the children into triangles, circles, and rectangles; and tomato cartons. String passed through two straws to form a rectangle also makes a good blower.
- The children will dip their blowers into the solution and blow bubbles.

BUBBLE SOLUTION

1 teaspoon glycerin

½ cup (125 ml) liquid detergent

½ cup (125 ml) water

Put glycerin, liquid detergent, and water into a 2-liter soda bottle. Shake well.

More

Do this activity outdoors on a cold day to observe how bubbles freeze as well as fly upward due to the warm air from the children's lungs. Mix a large amount of bubble solution in a plastic wading pool. Stand in the center of the pool and attempt to encapsulate your body with a bubble using a hula hoop. Don't want to get wet? Use the hula hoop to make enormous bubbles. Just dip it in the solution and wave it carefully.

Create and experiment with new bubble blowers.

Questions to assess language development

EXPRESSIVE LANGUAGE

Can the children direct you and their peers to blow, pop, make, and dip with a variety of action words?

Can the children describe the appearance and actions of the bubbles?

RECEPTIVE LANGUAGE

Can the children follow your directions to blow, pop, make, and dip their bubble makers?

Literacy Connections

READING EXPERIENCES

Bubble Bubble by Mercer Mayer

When a young boy buys a magic bubble maker, the bubbles get out of control.

WRITING EXPERIENCES

- Share the illustrations of Bubble Bubble, by Mercer Mayer. Invite children to dictate a story to go with the illustrations. Read the children's story back to them.

- Glue different-sized circles of colored cellophane on pages of small blank books. Children can complete the bubble illustrations and write or dictate stories to go with them. Read the completed books to the children, and place the books in the class library.

- Cut out the conversation "bubbles" from favorite comic strips. Invite children to write or dictate new dialogue for the comic strip characters. Read the finished comics to the children, then display them for children to refer to.

Pouring and Filling

The water table rates high as a child center choice. It's always a fun place to play and it presents an unlimited source of language and eye-hand coordination for all participants. Action words (verbs) that are not as commonly used can be modeled and elicited in this activity.

What you will need

Plastic bowls
Pitchers
Plastic cups
Paper cups
Funnels
Water source
Drop cloth
Paper towels
Water table or basin

Words you can use

cups	containers
bowls	funnel
pitcher	pour
fill	empty
in	out
slowly	fast
wet	messy
paper	hole
little	too much
help	over
under	stop
hold	

What to do

- Have a variety of unbreakable materials available at the water table (or large deep bowl or basin) such as various-sized bowls, plastic cups, paper cups with large holes, paper cups with small holes, paper cups with no holes, pitchers, and funnels
- Place the cups, pitcher, and other items near the water container.
- Let the children freely explore the play materials. Listen to them talking as they pour water to fill, empty, and refill containers.
- After the children have freely explored and interacted with the materials, you might ask them to identify and describe how they are using them.

More

Have the children utilize their pouring and filling skills at snack or lunch time.

Questions to assess language development

EXPRESSIVE LANGUAGE

Can the children use specific verbs and descriptors in their water play?

RECEPTIVE LANGUAGE

Can the children associate new verbs and descriptors with the actions they are engaging in?

Literacy Connections

WRITING EXPERIENCES

- Because this activity can result in "messy" play, encourage the children to dictate a list of rules for the use of the materials such as "Only two people at a time" and "Dry your hands on the towel." Post their list of rules in the center; refer to them frequently, and encourage the children to refer to them.

- Help the children record the results of their pouring and filling by making charts such as "two butter tubs fill up one cheese container." Use these charts as points of discussion.

- Encourage the children to write or dictate letters to their families explaining what they did in this activity. These letters can be sent home as a way to encourage similar water play at the kitchen sink or in the bathtub.

Highway in the Sand

Children enjoy building miniature cities and highways, and through this activity are encouraged to talk about the different kinds of transportation they have experienced or might like to experience.

What you will need

Sand/water table

Sand

Shovels

Scoops

Spoons

Toy vehicles

Plastic cups and glasses for sand molds

Words you can use

build	make
sand	highway
road	connect
hills	curves
cars	trucks
fast	slow
city	house
play	town
mold	go
shovel	spoon
sign	building

What to do

● Encourage the children to use spoons, scoops, shovels, and their hands to make highways in the sand.

● They can build towns or cities that are connected by the highways.

● Provide a variety of small toy vehicles.

More

Make tiny highway signs and place them at intersections, hills, and curves. Share pictures of stop signs and other signs for railroad crossings, caution, curve ahead, etc.

Children can make larger signs to use with wheel toys on the playground.

Questions to assess language development

EXPRESSIVE LANGUAGE

Can the children name items associated with travel?

Can the children elaborate to describe their actions or previous experiences?

Literacy Connections

READING EXPERIENCES

The Biggest Truck by David Lyon

Jim gets up when everyone else goes to sleep so he can get his load of strawberries delivered before morning.

Night Ride by Bernie Karlin and Mati Karlin

Billy and his mom drive all night from the city to the country, observing the night scenery along the way.

Truck Song by Diane Siebert

This book describes in rhyme what it's like to be in a big rig with a trucker on the road.

WRITING EXPERIENCES

● Assist the children in making road signs for their sand highways. Children may write or dictate words for their signs.

● Invite the children to make signs for the wheel toys on the playground. They could add signs for delivery vehicles, highway assistance, and police cars.

● If the class goes on a field trip, encourage the children to keep a log of things they see along the highway. They may draw or write in small blank books or on sheets held on clipboards.

Sand Table Landscaping

Playing in the sand offers limitless opportunities for the children to use both descriptive and expressive language. This activity provides yet another way to create, build, and have fun.

What you will need

Collecting bags

Items from nature

Sand

Water

Cups and plastic glasses for sand molds

Sand sifters

Words you can use

sand

build

landscape

mold

fill

make

feel

touch

house

design

collect

decorate

clean

sift

dampen

wet

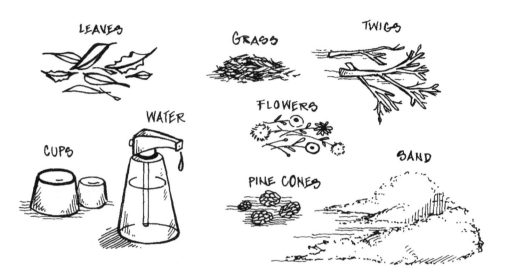

What to do

- Let the children gather a collection of leaves, grass, twigs, pinecones, and wildflowers such as violets, dandelions, and chickweed.
- Dampen the sand with water so it will support the items collected.
- Encourage the children to build a sand house. Cups or plastic glasses can be used as molds.
- Let the children create their own miniature backyards, decorating them as they wish with the collected items.
- The children can use sifters to clear the sand of the collected landscape materials when they are finished playing.

More

Build a sand park.

Questions to assess language development

EXPRESSIVE LANGUAGE

Can the children name items they are creating?

Can the children describe the landscapes they have created?

Literacy Connections

Building a House by Byron Barton

> Bulldozers and carpenters take readers through the entire process of building a house in this picture book.

Castle Builder by Dennis Nolan

> A small boy finds adventure by building a sand castle and then going inside it to conquer dragons.

The Little House by Virginia Lee Burton

> This is the classic story of a little house that survives the growth of the town around it.

This Is My House by Arthur Dorros

> Children from around the world describe their houses, including houseboats, caves, and yurts. Watercolor illustrations give detail to the descriptions.

WRITING EXPERIENCES

- Invite the children to draw and label plans for their landscapes.
- Make a class book titled "The Backyard Book." Invite the children to draw pictures of their backyards. Encourage them to write or dictate captions for their pages. Fasten the pages together. Read the book to the class, then place it in the class library.
- Glue photos of yards and gardens from magazines onto chart paper. Label each item in the photo as the children identify it.

Sand Drawing

Sand can be a very creative art medium for young children. This activity gives children the opportunity to design their own masterpieces as they explore another way to have fun in the sand. Vocabulary expansion is the language emphasis in this creative activity.

What you will need

Fine sand

White glue

Large box to catch excess sand

Drop cloth around the work area

Shakers such as salt shaker, oatmeal boxes with holes punched in the base, sugar shakers, cheese shakers

Words you can use

sand

glue

paste

fill

pour

lid

top

design

picture

make

box

feel

touch

look

spread

shake

more

squeeze

What to do

● Have the children squeeze white glue on a sheet of construction paper. They can make any picture or design they want.

● Let the children practice their motor skills as they pour sand to fill small shakers with larger holes.

● After shakers are filled, the children can shake their shakers so the sand comes out on their glue designs.

● Shake the papers over a box until the excess sand falls off the pasted paper.

More

Use colored sand.

Use flavored Jello in place of sand for scented creations.

Use shakers with varying hole sizes.

Questions to assess language development

Can the children label items and talk about their creations using appropriate, specific words?

Literacy Connections

WRITING EXPERIENCES

- Make tactile letter cards by printing each letter of the alphabet on an index card using glue. Pour colored sand over the glue and let dry. Put these cards in the writing center or the class library for the children to trace over with their fingers. They may also want to lay a blank sheet of thin paper over the letter and rub with the side of a crayon to create a crayon rubbing.

- Use glue on poster board to write some of the words the children use to describe their sand drawings. Then sprinkle colored sand or glitter over the glue. Hang the words up at the children's eye level. Read the words back to the children and encourage them to visit the poster to touch and reread the words.

- If the children use colored sand for their designs, encourage them to write or dictate a caption for their picture, such as "Amanda used red and blue sand" or "Nathan drew an alligator with green sand."

- Invite the children to make labels for the various shakers of sand, such as "Red Sand," or "Gold Glitter." Tape the labels onto the shakers and model reading them as you use them.

Water Drop Magnifier

Children enjoy playing and exploring with water. This activity gives them the opportunity to discover the magnification qualities of this vital liquid. Vocabulary words to discuss changes in what they see will be encouraged. Numbers and letters can also be named as viewed in the magnifiers.

What you will need

Pipettes
Water
Wax paper
Newspaper
Scissors

Words you can use

magnify
big
bigger
large
larger
look
observe
see
happens
size
predict
smaller
pipette
dropper
water

What to do

- Have the children cut wax paper into three-inch (eight-centimeter) squares.
- Give each child a piece of the wax paper.
- Have the children cut four-inch (ten-centimeter) squares of printed material from newspaper. Each child gets a square.
- Children cover the newspaper square with the piece of wax paper.
- Give each child a pipette (medicine dropper) and some water and ask them to place one drop of water on the wax paper.
- Observe closely and see what happens to the size of the print when viewed through the drop.

More

Place a piece of plastic wrap over an empty half-gallon plastic or paper bucket that has the bottom removed. (See illustration.) Secure with a rubber band. Place a small object in the bucket. Let the children look at the object in the bucket. Now pour a small amount of water on the plastic wrap. What happens as you look at the object through the water?

Questions to assess language development

EXPRESSIVE LANGUAGE

Can the children tell what changes they see?

Can the children name letters or numbers in the magnified print?

RECEPTIVE LANGUAGE

Can the children follow simple directives to act on the magnifiers such as look, drop water, and see?

Literacy Connections

READING EXPERIENCES

A Drop of Water by Walter Wick

This nonfiction book contains many photographs that magnify water in different forms, such as frost, ice, and steam.

WRITING EXPERIENCES

- Invite the children to write on a variety of sizes of paper, from three-inch (eight-centimeter) squares to large pieces of newsprint.
- Place magnifying glasses in the class library. Encourage the children to look at books through the glasses and talk about what happens when a magnifying glass is held over the pages.
- Take a print walk around the center or neighborhood. Encourage the children to point out print that is small and print that is large, such as on signs. Invite the children to illustrate a part of their walk, and to write or dictate a caption. Display the illustrations on the wall or in a class book.

Water Feelings and Looks

The water table is a great place for the children to express themselves regarding the sensations they have as they interact with any activity that is wet and messy. Use these moments to listen and interact to elicit both expressive and descriptive language.

What you will need

Water table

Objects that change when immersed in water

Objects that don't change other than getting wet

Words you can use

wet

change

feel

touch

bottom

under

hold

think

predict

dissolve

gone

disappear

soft

hard

names of objects

THINGS THAT CHANGED
dry sponge
liquid soap
sugar cube

THINGS THAT DID NOT
a marble
a child's hand
a pencil

What to do

- Gather a collection of objects that when immersed in water will feel and perhaps look different than before they were immersed.
- Ask the child to hold the object and describe how it feels such as hard, soft, shiny, and rough.
- Have the child place the object in the water and hold it under for a few seconds.
- When the object is removed from the water, have the child describe the change in appearance, if any, and the change as to how it feels.

More

Make drawings of objects when they are wet and when they are dry.

Classify and chart objects that change in appearance when they get wet.

Questions to assess language development

Can the children tell about and describe the object they are holding?

Can the children tell how the item changed?

Literacy Connections

READING EXPERIENCES

My Life With the Wave by Catherine Cowan

> A little boy goes to the ocean and brings home a wave, much to his family's surprise.

Until I Saw the Sea: A Collection of Seashore Poems edited by Alison Shaw

> Some of the greatest poets describe the beautiful sea and seashore in this collection of poems.

WRITING EXPERIENCES

● Make a chart to record the water experience. You may want to label two charts "Things That Changed" and "Things That Did Not Change." Encourage the children to talk about which items seemed to change when dipped in the water, and record their ideas. Read the chart together and occasionally refer to it throughout the day or week.

● Invite the children to write or draw on paper with washable markers. Have them quickly dip their finished pieces in a tub of water. Encourage them to talk about what happened. You may want them to predict what will happen before dipping the paper in water.

● Brush a piece of paper with clean water. Invite the children to write on the wet paper using a variety of instruments, such as markers, crayons, pens, and pencils. Encourage them to talk about the results.

● Children may want to use watercolors or fingerpaints because both are affected by the use of water. Allow the children to write and draw with either medium.

Look What I Found

Children hunt for familiar items buried in the sand. They use descriptive terms and labels as they identify their discoveries.

What you will need

Sand table, tub, or box

Dry sand, beans, or rice

Small objects to bury in the sand such as toy cars, buttons, pine cones

Metal objects and bingo wand magnets if using magnets

Words you can use

look

found

see

feel

cover

under

up

find

big

little

surprise

buried

MAGNETIC LETTER

WASHER

MAGNETIC FISH

What to do

● Place small familiar items in the sand and cover them.

● Invite the children to run their hands through the sand to see what they can find.

● Ask the children to raise the item from the sand and identify it.

More

Place metal objects in the sand (not too deeply) and pass a magnet close to the sand surface. As metal objects are attracted to the magnet they will jump from the sand and surprise the children. This will encourage the children to use descriptive and expressive language.

Before they lift the item from the sand, encourage the children to attempt to identify it by how it feels: "I feel a _____" or "It feels like _____."

Sort findings by size, color, and use. Match objects if buried in pairs.

Questions to assess language development

EXPRESSIVE LANGUAGE

Can the children name the items they find?

Can the children use descriptors for the items they find?

Literacy Connections

READING EXPERIENCES

Do You See a Mouse? by Bernard Waber

Everyone says there are no mice at the fancy Park Snoot Hotel, but the observant reader can find them hiding in the art.

Don't Tell the Whole World! by Joanna Cole

John finds a money box while he is plowing his field. It seems like good luck at first, but he worries his wife will tell their rich landlord about the money.

Nanta's Lion: A Search-and-Find Adventure by Audrey Wood

This is a great book to read aloud to preschoolers. They will enjoy finding the lion that Nanta is hunting.

WRITING EXPERIENCES

● Help children hide items around the room. Have them draw, write, or dictate directions for others to follow in order to find the items.

● Before hiding things in the sand, help children write descriptions of them for other children to read. The hunters can guess what they're looking for from the descriptions.

Measuring

Measuring can be taught as a pre-math skill, and the concepts and vocabulary utilized in math language can be introduced in play. Very basic items are targeted for both receptive and expressive use.

What you will need

Things to measure such as water, sand, dry cereal, rice, baking ingredients

Measuring cups

Words you can use

cup

measure

ingredients

enough

more

numbers

1, ½

measuring cup

small

big

large

smaller

larger

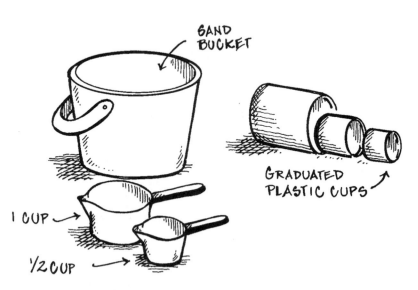

SAND BUCKET

GRADUATED PLASTIC CUPS

1 CUP

½ CUP

What to do

- Provide the children with measuring cups to play with in the water table. One cup and one-half cup sizes are good to start with. The one-half cup measure can be used to fill the larger cup. Big and little cups can be fun.
- While using different containers to measure, the children can also use measuring cups to fill up sand buckets, glasses, and other containers with water. Children can count how many cups they used to fill up various containers.
- Measure other things in the sand and water table such as cereal, sand, rice, or dirt.

More

Use a measuring cup to measure the amount of drink everyone gets.

Place cookbooks in the dramatic play center and the class library. Plan some simple cooking experiences using the cookbooks.

Questions to assess language development

EXPRESSIVE LANGUAGE

Can the children name the cups by modeling after the teacher or as they are prompted?

Can the children name the small or large containers?

Can the children rote count as they use a smaller container to fill a larger container?

RECEPTIVE LANGUAGE

Can the children find the various sizes of measuring cups as they are named or mentioned by the teacher?

Can the children identify the small or big containers?

Literacy Connections

READING EXPERIENCES

Inch by Inch by Leo Lionni

An inch worm saves his life by measuring a robin's tail and many of the robin's friends.

The Line-Up Book by Russo Marisabina

Before Sam goes to lunch, he lines up all his blocks, books, toys, and shoes to be able to reach the kitchen in one line.

WRITING EXPERIENCES

- Have the children create charts to show how many glasses of water fill up the bucket or how many little cups fill up a glass.

- Invite the children to write or dictate recipes for mud pies and other imaginary foods.

Opposites

The concept of opposites can lead to the use of adjectives in the language of young children. This activity gives children an experiential chance to explore early developing polar opposites such as up/down, big/little, clean/dirty, on/under, empty/full, and in/on.

What you will need

Sand/water table

Sand or water

Small containers such as paper cups, coffee measurers, small tea sets

Words you can use

clean

empty

small

dirty

big

smaller

on

bigger

smallest

under

biggest

up

full

little

down

PLASTIC ANIMALS

PAPER CUPS

TOY HELICOPTER

COFFEE MEASURERS

SMALL TEA SET

TOY PEOPLE

TOY CAR

What to do

- Provide children at the sand/water table with various containers such as cups, coffee measurers, and small tea sets.
- Prompt the children in their play to fill/empty the big/little containers, to lift them up/down as they fill them, to dump them in the water side of the table to experience clean/dirty, and to put them on/under the sand or water.
- As the children go through the various play motions, they are encouraged to name the appropriate polar opposite.

More

Plastic dolls or action figures can be used instead of various containers. They can be positioned in/out, under/on, etc.

Questions to assess language development

EXPRESSIVE LANGUAGE

Can the children name the appropriate polar opposite as they play?

RECEPTIVE LANGUAGE

Can children follow directions that involve polar opposites?

Literacy Connections

READING EXPERIENCES

Big and Little by Steve Jenkins

Through cut-paper collages, the author/illustrator presents animals found all around the world in a wide variety of sizes. He compares the animals to each other showing big and little.

Demi's Opposites: An Animal Game Book by Demi

Using brilliant color and rhyme, this book asks readers to search the illustrations to find opposites.

Exactly the Opposite by Tana Hoban

In this book, many opposites are illustrated in a series of photos.

What the Moon Saw by Brian Wildsmith

Using a series of opposites, the sun shows the moon many things to be found in the world.

WRITING EXPERIENCES

● Help the children write lists of opposites, either independently or as a class.

● Invite the children to write opposite riddles. On one side of a page they draw and write a word that has an opposite. On the back they draw and illustrate the opposite. They can share their riddles with friends, or put them in a class book to be placed in the class library.

● Children can hide objects in the class and write clues using opposites. For example, if something is hidden *in* a drawer, the clue will say it is *out*.

Wash the Dishes

Pretend play that involves familiar household activities has long been a favorite of young children. This activity allows children to pretend they are doing a household chore that they normally are not allowed to perform independently. Modeling and sequencing are important here, as well as encouraging vocabulary growth.

What you will need

Sand/water table

Water

Dishes and plastic glasses

Silverware

Sponge and soap (real or play)

Kitchen towel

Washcloth

Words you can use

wash	plate
knife	dry
bowl	fork
soap	cup
spoon	cloth
saucer	sponge
wet	soapy
clean	dry
begin	finish

Questions to assess language development

EXPRESSIVE LANGUAGE

Can the children name the items they are using?

RECEPTIVE LANGUAGE

Can the children find each item as you name it?

What to do

- Set up the sand and water table with the necessary items to "wash" dishes.

- Invite the children to pretend to wash and dry the dishes, glasses, and silverware. Continue as long as the children are interested. You might facilitate language by naming various dishes and silverware, as well as the items used to wash the dishes.

- After the children have played for a while, try making some playful mistakes, such as not providing water for washing, or attempting to dry "dirty" dishes. This should be done in a fun way, with the idea that the children will enjoy seeing your mistake and correcting it.

Literacy Connections

READING EXPERIENCES

Feast for Ten by Cathryn Falwell

What does it take to make a feast for ten people? Shopping, cooking, setting the table—everyone helps and soon the feasting begins.

WRITING EXPERIENCES

- Help the children write directions for washing dishes. Hang the directions near the sand and water table or the dramatic play area and refer to them regularly.

- Have blank books available for the children to draw and write in or dictate about various uses for different dishes. Children may want to write about silly things to do with dishes, such as wear a bowl for a hat or catch bugs with spoons.

- Help the children inventory the dramatic play center and make a chart of the dishes that are there. Hang the chart in the center as a check when putting things away.

Music and Movement

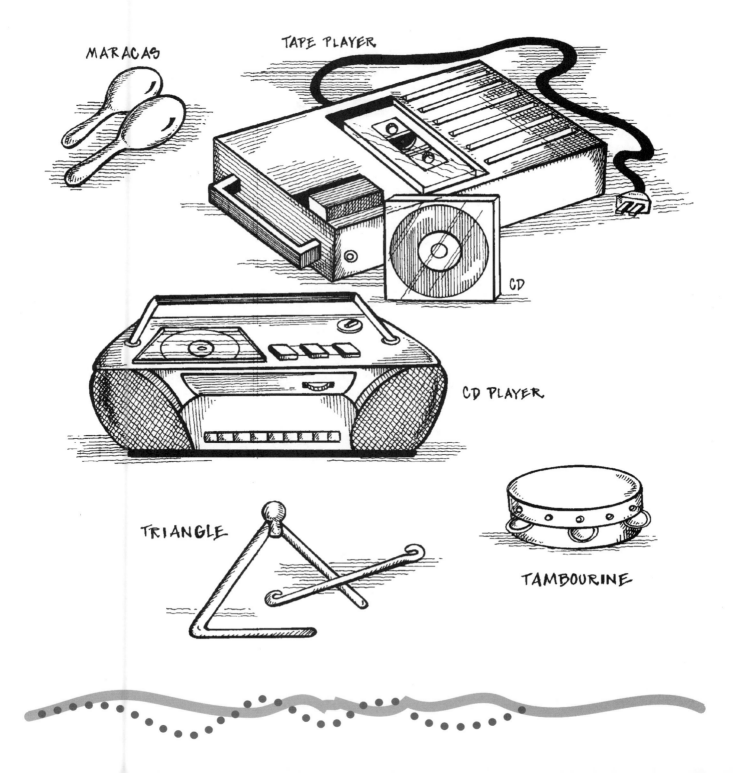

MARACAS

TAPE PLAYER

CD

CD PLAYER

TRIANGLE

TAMBOURINE

Kitchen Band

From a variety of kitchen utensils, the children choose instruments to play and keep tempo to recorded marching music. This noisy activity presents many opportunities for descriptive language in terms of sound and sound makers. Auditory discrimination skills will also be practiced.

Words you can use

Kitchen cooking utensils that produce sound when struck together

Marching band music

Words you can use

march

band

rhythm

loud

soft

high

low

play

leader

director

baton

pitch

noise

quiet

kitchen

music

bang

boom

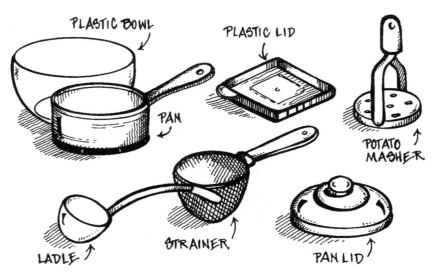

PLASTIC BOWL

PLASTIC LID

PAN

POTATO MASHER

LADLE

STRAINER

PAN LID

What to do

- The children choose a rhythm instrument from a collection of kitchen items such as metal spoons, wooden spoons, pots, pans, metal lids, and plastic bowls.
- The children take turns being the leader of the band.
- Play a taped march on the recorder. The children march around the room and play to the tempo of the music.
- Talk about the tempo of the march. Is it fast or slow?
- Invite the children to play softly and then loudly.

More

Have the band play to rock, jazz, and waltz music.

Questions to assess language development

RECEPTIVE LANGUAGE

Can children identify kitchen utensils by name?

Can children identify kitchen utensils by sound?

Can children adjust their "music making" to the various tempos of the recorded music?

Literacy Connections

READING EXPERIENCES

All Join In by Quentin Blake

Seven poems of children making noise, including wonderful music using kitchen pans!

Mama Don't Allow by Thacher Hurd

The swamp band, lead by Possum Miles, enjoys playing for a group of alligators. That is, until the band finds out what's planned for dinner!

Thump, Thump, Rat-a-Tat-Tat by Gene Baer

As the band gets closer and closer, it gets louder and louder and brighter and brighter. Finally the band is marching by.

WRITING EXPERIENCES

- Help children write a letter home requesting families to send different kinds of items to the class to use as musical instruments.

- Invite children to create their own music by writing or dictating the sequence of instruments to be played. For example, on chart paper, they may write "pan, pan, jar, jar, jar, spoons, pan, spoons, bowl." Help the children play their songs by reading the chart and indicating when each should play an instrument.

Junky Funky Music

Many items around the house can be recycled and used to create music and fun for the entire family. This activity is appropriate for both the home and the center. Listening skills with an emphasis on auditory recognition are at work in this fun activity.

What you will need

Empty toilet paper tubes

Wax paper

Scissors

Rubber bands

Shoeboxes

35mm film canisters

Rice

Popcorn kernals

Dried beans

Words you can use

music

tune

song

play

listen

hear

recycle

reuse

instrument

identify

name

blow

hum

shake

strike

strum

What to do

● Two weeks before starting the activity, send a note home to the parents requesting that they save and send to the center empty toilet paper rolls, 35mm film cannisters, and shoeboxes.

● Make the instruments following the instructions below.

TOILET PAPER ROLL KAZOO

Cut wax paper into a square large enough to cover the end of a toilet paper tube. Secure it over the end with a rubber band. To play, place your mouth over the open end of the tube and hum.

BOX GUITAR

Remove the lid from the shoebox and stretch three rubber bands across it. To play, strum the rubber bands.

SOUND SHAKERS

Give each child two film canisters. Place a small amount of popcorn kernals, rice, and beans in each canister and secure the lid. To play, shake the canisters.

- Play a familiar children's song with the toilet paper roll kazoo. Tell the children to listen carefully to see if they can name the tune that you are playing.
- The children can work in small groups of three or four to decide what instrument to make and what tune to play as part of a "Name That Tune" game.
- Invite the small groups to play their tunes and, after each one, the players should ask the other children to "Name that tune!"
- The other children can take turns trying to name the tune.
- Send home instructions for making homemade musical instruments or send home materials and instructions in an activity-lending bag.

More

Have a class band. Let the children play for other children in the center.

Children and parents can make instruments at a family meeting and play the "Name That Tune" game with their family members.

Children can use their instruments and parade around the room, center, or playground.

Literacy Connections

READING EXPERIENCES
. . . .

Crash! Bang! Boom! by Peter Spier

This book has picture and sound combinations that make it a great read aloud.

The Happy Hedgehog Band by Martin Waddell

Four hedgehogs make drums and form a band in the woods. Each drum makes a different sound, creating delightful music.

WRITING EXPERIENCES
. . . .

- Help children write letters home requesting families to send in items to be used when making instruments.
- Make a class book titled "How to Make Music." Invite each child to draw and write or dictate directions for making musical instruments out of junk material. Staple pages together and read the finished book to the class. Place the book in the class library when finished.

Questions to assess language development

EXPRESSIVE LANGUAGE
. . . .

Can children name the various items they are using to make their "instruments?"

Can children give one another directions to play together as a "band?"

RECEPTIVE LANGUAGE
. . . .

Can children identify songs played by the teacher on the "sample" instruments?

Move and Groove

Preschoolers enjoy learning to sing songs with accompanying movements. Three's and four's enjoy simple movements (e.g. clapping hands, turning around) while the five's utilize more complex motor skills (e.g. skipping, hopping). Listening to, singing along, and responding to movement instructions from the teacher, another child, or from those given on the record, tape, or CD that is being played provide an excellent opportunity for listening, language development, and motor skill development.

What you will need

Words and music to some simple action songs

Words you can use

move

dance

listen

hear

lyrics to song

What to do

● Start with an easy singing and doing activity such as "Itsy Bitsy Spider" and "The Ants Go Marching." The song should be one that has a number of small repetitive movements and words.

● Play or sing the song for the children.

● Play the song a second time and have the children try some of the movements with you. Encourage the children to make the movements any way that they wish (not just to imitate you) and to join in the singing as they do the movements.

More

Try a variety of songs.

Send words, music, and instructions home with the children so they can show and talk with their families about what they are learning.

Questions to assess language development

Can children sing and say the words to the chosen song as they "move and groove" to the music?

RECEPTIVE LANGUAGE

Can children attend and listen to the song that is chosen?

Literacy Connections

READING EXPERIENCES

See the list of songs made into picture books in the *Singing Helpers* activity. Additional picture book songs include:

Fiddle-I-Fee: A Farmyard Song for the Very Young by Melissa Sweet

I Know an Old Lady Who Swallowed a Fly by Glen Rounds

This Old Man by Carol Jones

The Three Little Kittens by Lorinda Bryan Cauley

WRITING EXPERIENCES

- Invite children to draw to different kinds of music. For example, they may draw "fast" pictures and "slow" pictures according to the tempo of the music. Encourage them to write or dictate captions for their drawings. Display the captioned drawings and refer to them throughout the week.

- Make a graph of the children's favorite music. On chart paper, list the words to describe some of the songs they sing and move to throughout the week. They may list words such as *fast, slow, loud,* and *soft.* Invite them to write their names beside the word or words that describe their favorite music.

Weather Moves

This activity gives the children an opportunity to respond with descriptive words and movement to their feelings and mind images as they listen to seasonal music.

What you will need

Seasonal CD Music, such as the following:

WINTER:

"Winter Daydreams" Symphony No. 1 in G minor, op. 13 by Peter Tchaikovsky, and Christmas music

SPRING AND SUMMER:

"Enchanted Garden" by Kevin Kern

ALL SEASONS:

"The Four Seasons" by Antonio Vivaldi

AUTUMN:

"Falling Leaves" by Nat King Cole

Words you can use

summer

fall

winter

spring

mood descriptors such as happy, sad

words associated with the various seasons such as windy, hot, warm, cold, cool, freezing, chilly, shiver

What to do

- Play a tape, record, or CD.
- Let the children move to the way the music makes them feel.
- Talk about their movements and the emotions that they feel as they hear spring, summer, fall, and winter music themes.
- Invite them to describe what they see as they listen.

More

Play short excerpts of various kinds of music and let the children respond verbally as to what they feel and see as they listen.

Questions to assess language development

EXPRESSIVE LANGUAGE

Can children say the descriptive words associated with the music?

RECEPTIVE LANGUAGE

Can children listen and attend to the various types of music being presented?

Literacy Connections

READING EXPERIENCES

Did You Hear Wind Sing Your Name? by Sandra De Coteau Orie

This beautifully illustrated song of the Oneida tribe celebrates the season of Spring.

Rain Talk by Mary Serfozo

You can almost feel the rain as you read the rain sounds and look at the watercolor illustrations in this lovely picture book.

Windsongs and Rainbows by Albert Burton

Beautiful language brings alive the sun, the wind, the rain, and the storm.

WRITING EXPERIENCES

- Invite children to draw scenes of themselves in different weather. Encourage them to write or dictate captions for their drawings.

- Keep a weather chart for a week. As children use words to describe the day's weather, write them on a chart. Refer to the chart throughout the day to see if words need to be added or changed.

- Have small blank books available for children to write and draw about their feelings and actions in different kinds of weather. For example, books may be titled "Windy Days," "Hot Days," and "Stormy Days."

Monkey in the Middle

A circular version of "Follow the Leader" allows children to see and hear directions, as well as model the actions of a peer. Children are allowed to lead in a non-demanding way in this motor activity. Initiation is important as a conversational skill, and this nonverbal play activity sets up the context for the child to succeed.

What you will need

Large space
Motor movement ideas

Words you can use

march
swing
bend
kneel
stomp
spin
jump
kick
dance
shake
wiggle
walk
jumping jack
run in place

What to do

● The children form a circle in a large area in the outdoor play area (or indoor gross motor area in inclimate weather).
● One child goes to the middle of the circle and becomes the "Monkey in the Middle."
● He names a gross motor action such as marching, swinging arms, and touching toes, and models for the others in the circle. This is the "initiation" opportunity for each child.
● The other children follow the action of the leader.
● After one or two minutes, the "monkey" is changed until all children have had a turn to be the leader.

More

Action combinations such as spinning in a circle or kneeling can be incorporated into the activity. The actions will still need to be named if possible. Sequencing can also be incorporated here if the child does one action first and another last!

Questions to assess language development

EXPRESSIVE LANGUAGE

Can children name the action they want the others in the group to copy?

How are the children at taking the initiator role? If some children are more reluctant, they may be able to go into the middle with a buddy!

Literacy Connections

READING EXPERIENCES

Caps for Sale by Esphyr Slobodkina

In this classic tale, monkeys steal all the caps from a peddler while he sleeps.

Five Little Monkeys Sitting in a Tree by Eileen Christoleow

A follow-up to *Five Little Monkeys Jumping on the Bed*, the young monkeys in this story are going to get snapped up by a hungry crocodile if they're not careful!

Monkey See, Monkey Do by Marc Gave

When monkeys come to visit, they cause problems with their antics.

WRITING EXPERIENCES

● Make a chart for children to record the "monkey business" portrayed in the game. For example, "Missy jumped up and down. Nathan crawled on his knees." Read and reread the finished chart, and refer to the chart regularly for several days.

● Have small blank books available for children to illustrate things they or their friends can do. Invite them to write words to describe their actions, such as, "I can hop on one foot."

● Make a class alphabet book of actions children can do. Help children think of things they can do that start with different letters of the alphabet. Write their words and let them illustrate their pages.

Follow Me

Listening, watching, following directions, and spatial relations are all emphasized in this activity as children play "Follow the Leader" on the playground equipment.

What you will need

Playground equipment and other objects such as wagons and boxes

Words you can use

up/down

over/under

in/out

top/bottom

through

around

between

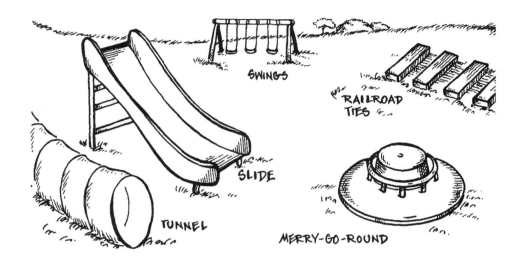

What to do

- Children form a line behind the "leader" on the playground.
- The leader takes her followers through various pieces of playground equipment announcing the body position they must assume as they move through the equipment. (For example, she might tell them to go *under* the slide, go *around* the merry-go-round, go *through* the tunnel, and climb *over* the railroad tie.)
- All children repeat the body position as they move through the pieces of playground equipment.
- The leader changes after five movements through the equipment.

More

If inclement weather, use indoor equipment or classroom furniture such as tables, chairs, and bookcases.

Questions to assess language development

EXPRESSIVE LANGUAGE

Can the "leader" verbalize the directions for her group to follow?

RECEPTIVE LANGUAGE

Can children follow the directions as they are announced and modeled by the "leader?"

Literacy Connections

READING EXPERIENCES

Make Way for Ducklings by Robert McClosky

> The little ducklings follow their mother everywhere, and traffic comes to an amusing halt when they follow her across the street.

Too Much by Dorothy Stott

> Little Duck tries to swim in places no one would want to follow, including a pickle jar and a sink full of dishes. Finally he ends up in the pond.

Up the Wall by Nicholas Heller

> When there's nowhere else to play, the narrator takes a bag of toys and food, along with the dog, and climbs up the wall to the ceiling. There's plenty of space on the ceiling, even though everything is upside down.

WRITING EXPERIENCES

- Help the children draw and label a simple map of where a leader took them.
- Encourage children to draw, write, or dictate "Follow Me" tales describing where they would like the class to follow them.
- Make an experience chart about the following adventure. As children describe where the leader took them, write their words. Reread the chart throughout the day, and encourage children to reread it with you and on their own.

Backwards Fun

This activity helps children to understand and use opposite words. If coordinated with music, the children can have a great time while practicing an important concept. When the activity is targeting a word during music, the children may listen exceptionally close to be sure they catch the "backward" word.

What you will need

Carpet squares
Music book

Words you can use

stand/sit
loud/soft
hot/cold
clean/dirty
happy/sad
fast/slow
open/close
thick/thin
night/day
up/down
on/off
full/empty

HEAD, SHOULDERS, KNEES and TOES

OLD MacDONALD'S

ABC

IF YOU'RE SAD and YOU KNOW IT, CLAP YOUR HANDS

What to do

- Come into an area for singing, perhaps the circle time area with the rugs.

- Begin to use opposites right away, telling the children that you are going to need some help as you are feeling "backwards." Have them sit down for music time, and then remain standing and say "Everyone sitting, OK, I'm sitting too." The children should prompt you that you are still standing and let you know you are "backwards." Act surprised and allow them to guide you to the "opposite" of what you are doing.

- Begin the music period, choosing a song with lots of possibilities for opposites. "Head, Shoulders, Knees, and Toes" can be done in reverse order, "Old MacDonald's" animals can be making the wrong sounds, and the "ABC" song can begin with the letter Z. You can also tell the children know that you are going to sing "softly" and then burst out in a loud song.

- The children should thoroughly enjoy themselves as they "catch" you being backwards.

More

The children can choose a familiar song that they can lead with their peers, inserting "backwards" words as they sing.

You can make any period during the day "backwards" time, or have an entire "backwards" day.

Questions to assess language development

EXPRESSIVE LANGUAGE

Can children say certain words, and then act "backwards?"

RECEPTIVE LANGUAGE

Are children able to "catch" you doing the opposite of what you are saying?

Literacy Connections

READING EXPERIENCES

Silly Sally by Audrey Wood

"Silly Sally went to town, walking backward, upside down." Playful pictures and rollicking rhyme sweep listeners along on Sally's journey.

The following backwards activities help focus children's attentions on the directionality of reading:

- Let children catch you reading while holding a book upside down.

- Begin a favorite story such as *Brown Bear, Brown Bear, What Do You See?* at the end. Invite children to help you continue reading the story backwards.

- Use a big book of a familiar story. On one page, begin reading the sentence backwards, pointing to the words as your read. Ask children to tell you what's wrong.

- Write the children's names backwards. Ask them if they notice any difference. Then hold the paper up to a mirror for children to see the difference.

- Make special name tags for the day with children's last names printed on them instead of their first names. Read these name tags and ask children to identify who they belong to.

Dance Party

Moving to the rhythm of music is fun and beneficial to children's motor development. Coordination and relaxation is achieved as the body responds to the beat of the music. Free dancing may be expressed by jumping, whirling, twisting, and gliding or any other movements that the music suggests. Movement and action words are modeled as everyone "dances."

What you will need

Record, disc, or tape player

Music such as waltz, rock, country western, and classical music

Words you can use

dance

move

rhythm

music

body

ribbon

jumping

galloping

walking

whirling

hopping

loud

soft

play

What to do

- Play a variety of music on discs or tapes.
- Tell the children that you are going to play some music and invite them all to listen.
- Give each child a ribbon, streamer, or strip of crepe paper. Demonstrate how they can be moved to the rhythm of the music.
- Tell the children that they can dance and listen at the same time. Let the children move and sway to the music as they wave their ribbons.

More

Play marches and let the children march to the music using a variety of march steps such as high steps, long stretching steps, side steps, backward steps.

Questions to assess language development

Can children put a name to the action they are doing?

RECEPTIVE LANGUAGE

Can children attend to the music?

Can children pick up the "rhythm" of the music?

Literacy Connections

READING EXPERIENCES

Barn Dance! by Bill Martin, Jr. and John Archambault

> On a full-moon night, a young boy sneaks out to the barn to find the animals holding a barn dance.

Color Dance by Ann Jonas

> Three children use scarves while dancing and make different colors as their red, blue, and yellow scarves overlap.

The Moon Jumpers by Janice May Udry

> Four children enjoy dancing in the moonlight.

WRITING EXPERIENCES

- Play music softly while the children write in journals, blank books, or blank paper. Encourage children to talk about their writing.

- Have available blank books for children to draw, write, or dictate about how things move, and give them titles such as "Fast Things" and "Slow Things."

- Invite children to draw to music. Then invite them to write or dictate captions for their drawings.

Quiet Time

Music can create a variety of feelings and emotions. Using it to slow down and relax is an excellent way to move into nap time and/or rest time.

What you will need

Books
Puzzles
Record or tape player
Soft relaxing listening music

Words you can use

rest
sleep
time
listen
soft
quiet
slow
tired
whisper
alone
nap
music

What to do

● Let the children select a book or puzzle to take to their individual rest area.
● As they recline and look at their book or work their puzzle, they begin to slow down and relax.
● Play soft music to further set the mood. Some children will not sleep but will get needed rest as they take a break from their active daily routine.
● Soft words and relaxing music such as lullabies can contribute to slowing children down for quiet time.

More

Read stories about animals and then suggest that the children mimic an animal position to rest in.

Questions to assess language development

Can children attend to the sounds of the music?

Literacy Connections

READING EXPERIENCES

Going to Sleep on the Farm by Wendy Cheyette Lewison

> Watercolor illustrations and chantable refrains engage the children in this story of a dad and his son as they talk about how animals sleep while playing with miniature toy animals.

The Napping House by Audrey Wood

> In this cumulative story, everyone's sleeping in the napping house until a wakeful flea bites the mouse, who wakes the cat. . . .

Naptime, Laptime by Eileen Spinelli

> This rhyming story shows how animals sleep—from snakes who "drowse upon a rock," to spiders "in the kitchen clock."

Sleep Tight by B.G. Hennessy

> A rhyming description of the many things sleeping, such as animals in the yard and toys on the shelf.

WRITING EXPERIENCES

- Invite children to take paper and pencil to their rest areas. They may wish to write or draw while resting. Encourage children to share their writings after rest time.

Let's Make Some Noise

Sounds (noises) are encountered by children everyday. Listening to the different sounds and discriminating the source from which they originated can result in descriptive vocabulary as well as ear training to sharpen sound discrimination.

What you will need

Drawing, picture, or model of
    an ear

Tape recorder

Words you can use

sound

noise

listen

hear

ear

loud

soft

house

outdoors

tape recorder

names of rooms in the center

names of indoor and outdoor
    sound sources

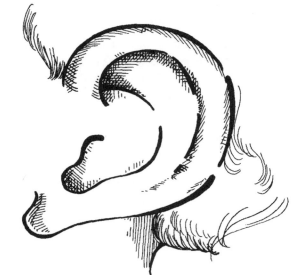

What to do

- Ask the children to tell how we can hear sounds and noises.
- Show a poster board drawing or cut out of an ear. Tell the children that when you hold up the ear, they should all be as quiet as possible and listen carefully to the sounds around them. Then when you put the ear behind your back, encourage the children to share the sounds that they heard while listening.
- Repeat the listening exercise three or four times in different areas of the classroom and center as additional sounds may be detected.
- Talk about the sounds they heard and where they feel the sounds are coming from. Do this in each room following the careful listening.

More

Do the same activity outdoors.

Make a tape recording with the child walking from area to area and tapping sounds such as a telephone ringing, answering machine, door closing, toilet flushing, alarm ringing, and radio playing.

Take a walk around the center and use a wooden spoon to tap on different surfaces. Talk about the different sound that each surface makes when it is tapped.

Questions to assess language development

EXPRESSIVE LANGUAGE

Can children name the sources of sounds they hear?

RECEPTIVE LANGUAGE

Can children attend to sounds?

Can children differentiate sounds?

Can children localize sound (figure out where the source of the sound is)?

Literacy Connections

READING EXPERIENCES

At Mary Bloom's by Aliki

A little girl wants to call her friend, but is afraid that Mary Bloom's animals will create too much noise.

Meet the Marching Smithereens by Ann Hayes

A lively marching band of animals introduces the reader to facts about brass, percussion, and woodwind instruments.

Poems Go Clang: A Collection of Noisey Verse by Debi Gliori

This collection of rowdy rhymes features sounds of all kinds.

Polar Bear, Polar Bear, What Do You Hear? by Bill Martin, Jr.

Using a familiar pattern, this version uses animal sounds like a hippo snorting.

WRITING EXPERIENCES

- Help children make a chart of Inside Sounds/Outside Sounds by listing the things the children hear.

- Encourage children to carry a clipboard or notebook to write down the things they hear throughout the day. Invite them to write or draw the things they hear in different areas of the school or center.

Quick as a Cricket

This activity title reflects a children's book entitled *Quick as a Cricket* by Audrey Wood. This book is full of metaphors, one of the structures children learn as they develop figurative language. The book pictures can serve as models for children as they move "like a _____." This activity also builds vocabulary for descriptive words in an enjoyable manner.

What you will need

Quick as a Cricket by Audrey Wood

Words you can use

quick	cricket
slow	snail
small	ant
large	whale
sad	basset
happy	lark
nice	bunny
mean	shark
cold	hot
weak	strong
loud	quiet
tough	gentle
brave	shy
tame	wild
lazy	busy
toad	fox
kitten	ox
lion	clam
rhino	lamb
tiger	shrimp
poodle	chimp
lizard	bee

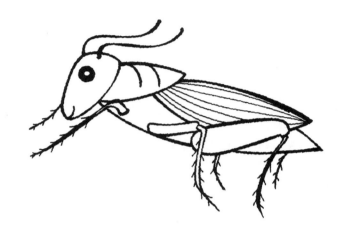

What to do

● Read *Quick as a Cricket* by Audrey Wood to the children.
● Invite the children to choose which animal they want to "act out" according to the pictures and descriptions in the book.
● Children take turns acting out the description of various animals from the book. They will label the descriptor and the animal they are acting out.

More

Children can incorporate the sounds made by various animals.

Children can categorize various animals according to type, where they live, how they have their babies (eggs vs. mammals), and other characteristics.

Questions to assess language development

EXPRESSIVE LANGUAGE

Can children name the movement they are performing?

Can children label the animal they are imitating?

RECEPTIVE LANGUAGE

Can children listen and attend to the story being read aloud?

Can the children pattern their movements as described in the book?

Literacy Connections

READING EXPERIENCES

Five Minutes Peace by Jill Murphy

> A mother elephant tries to find some peace and quiet, but her three children do what they can to see that this doesn't happen.

My Many Colored Days by Dr. Seuss

> "Some days are yellow. Some are blue. On different days I'm different too." The rhyming story goes on to describe how different feelings are all part of being who we are.

The Very Quiet Cricket by Eric Carle

> A repetitive refrain involves the readers in this story of a cricket who can't make a sound until he meets an equally quiet female cricket.

WRITING EXPERIENCES

- Have available small blank books for children to draw in and write about how different animals move. Invite them to use descriptive words such as those found in *Quick as a Cricket.*

- Make charts with the children listing things that make them feel happy or sad, nice or mean. Hang the charts around the room and reread them occasionally.

Where Would You Hide
if You Were the Gingerbread Man?

Children enjoy this old favorite. This activity gives them the opportunity to be creative and to fantasize about what they might do if they were in the Gingerbread Man's position. Beginning narrative abilities such as the language skills involved in relating setting, characters, and story line are the emphasis here.

What you will need

Poster board

Newsprint

Drawing paper

Crayons

Pencil

"The Gingerbread Man,"
   any version

Words you can use

hide

tell

find

run

draw

write

describe

hiding place

What to do

- Read a version of the classic tale, "The Gingerbread Man."
- Make a drawing of the Gingerbread Man on a large piece of poster board or newsprint.
- Ask the children where they would hide if they were the Gingerbread Man.
- As the children respond, write their descriptions on the drawing.

More

Write the children's dictation on their own drawings. Encourage the children to use inventive spelling to write their hiding place descriptions.

Questions to assess language development

EXPRESSIVE LANGUAGE

Can children respond to the "where" question appropriately?

RECEPTIVE LANGUAGE

Can children listen and attend as the story is read aloud to them?

Literacy Connections

READING EXPERIENCES

The Gingerbread Boy by Richard Egielski

This new telling of an old tale places the gingerbread boy on a big city street, and his chasers include construction workers, street musicians, and a policeman.

You Can't Catch Me by Charlotte Doyle

This book captures the wonderful excitement of the game of chase, where getting away is never as much fun as getting caught.

WRITING EXPERIENCES

After reading and responding to "The Gingerbread Man," invite children to participate in some of the following literacy extensions:

- Make some gingerbread. Put the recipe on a chart and read it with the children while each step is completed.

- Read several versions of "The Gingerbread Man." Involve the children in a discussion about the differences and similarities among the different versions.

- Using clothespins and string, hang illustrations of several events from the story in order. Have the children retell the story from the illustrations. Mix up the illustrations and invite the children to hang them back in the correct order.

- Hide gingerbread men cookie cutters or actual cookies wrapped in plastic wrap throughout the room. On a chart or on a series of index cards, write simple clues to finding the cookie cutters. Read the clues with the children and invite them to find the gingerbread man.

Singing Helpers

This activity puts a new twist on transition or clean-up times. The children are encouraged to sing creative tunes as they go about their clean-up routine. Putting words to music helps children follow their own movements as they play.

What you will need

Songbook with familiar
   children's tunes

Words you can use

children's names

routine words for familiar
   actions of the day

What to do

● Encourage children to pick a familiar tune such as the "ABC Song," "Itsy-Bitsy Spider," or "Jingle Bells." Hum the tune with the group to be sure the children have some idea of what the song sounds like.

● Demonstrate to the children how you begin to clean up for transition by singing "Miss Cindy picks up one toy, one toy, one toy" to the tune of "Johnny Bangs With One Hammer." Encourage the children to join in, singing their own names.

● Have the children pick another song, then change the words to include their own names doing whatever chores have become their routine.

More

Use "singing chores" format for line-up, snack times, going home, etc.

Questions to assess language development

EXPRESSIVE LANGUAGE

Do children sing the words that go with each chosen song?

Can children put new words into songs?

READING EXPERIENCES

Can children identify tunes from a "humming" version without words?

Literacy Connections

READING EXPERIENCES

Many favorite children's songs have been published in picture books. The titles listed below are a few to choose from to read and sing with the children.

The Farmer in the Dell by Kathy Parkinson

Take Me Out to the Ballgame by Jack Norworth

Today Is Monday by Eric Carle

The Wheels on the Bus by Maryann Kovalski

WRITING EXPERIENCES

- Create small books that have the words from one of the children's favorite songs, but leave blanks for the children to fill in their own words. For example, write "Today is Monday. Today is Monday. Monday _____." Children can write or dictate a food they like. Do the same for Tuesday, Wednesday, and so on. Invite children to illustrate their books.

- Let children choose which area of the room they will be responsible for during clean-up time. Have them write their names on a chart indicating their area. When a clean-up song begins, refer to the chart to remind them what they are to do.

Math

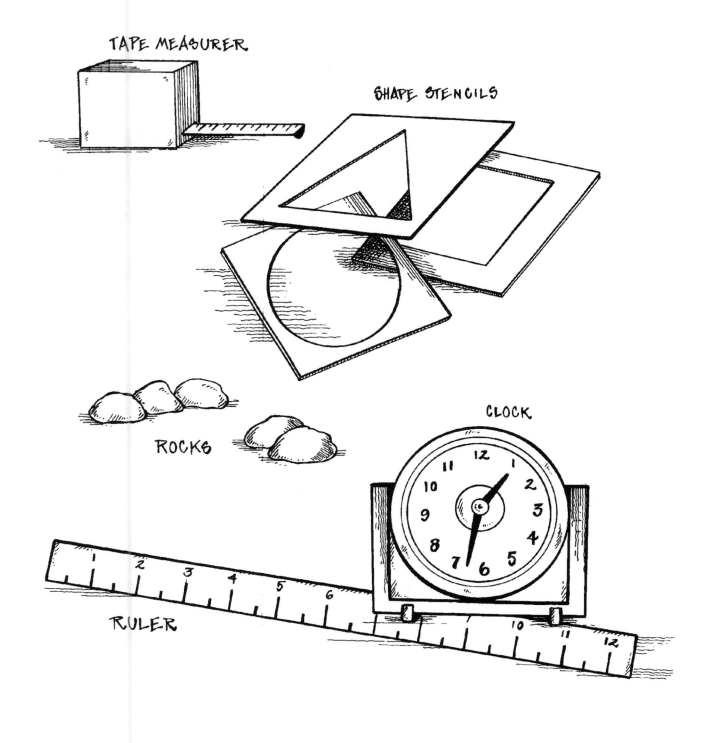

TAPE MEASURER

SHAPE STENCILS

ROCKS

CLOCK

RULER

Shape Bingo

Use this developmentally appropriate game to practice matching skills, auditory listening, and discrimination skills.

What you will need

Poster board
Markers
Bingo chips

Words you can use

cover
line
circle
round
triangle
three sides
square
four sides
equal
rectangle
oval
other shapes words

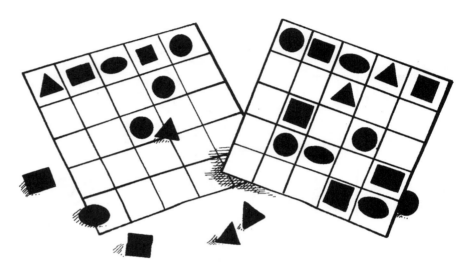

What to do

● Make bingo cards with different shapes on them. Use circles, ovals, squares, rectangles, and triangles.
● Make large cards with one shape on each.
● Use real bingo chips or pieces of paper cut into small circles.
● Play shape bingo. Hold up one shape card or with older children call out different shapes.
● The children put a bingo chip on one of the shapes on their card that has been called. The children play until everyone gets a row of bingo.

More

Children can take turns being the bingo caller.
Instead of shapes, make bingo cards with different colors or numbers.

Questions to assess language development

EXPRESSIVE LANGUAGE

Can children call out "bingo" when they realized they have a certain section of their card covered?

RECEPTIVE LANGUAGE

Can children identify the various shapes by name as they are called out in the game?

Literacy Connections

READING EXPERIENCES

Grandfather Tang's Story by Ann Tompert

Grandfather Tang uses tangrams to show each character as he tells his granddaughter a story. Illustrations include a black tangram diagram that shows how to arrange the tangrams into each animal.

A Pair of Socks by Stuart J. Murphy

This simple, colorful story teaches the basic math concept of matching.

WRITING EXPERIENCES

- Have available a variety of blank books cut into shapes. Children can draw, write, or dictate about things they see that are the same shape as the book.

- Invite children on a Shape Hunt. Give children a clipboard or a piece of heavy cardboard with a spring clip on top to hold paper. Go on a trip around the room, building, or yard and have children draw or write the names of things they see that are a certain shape. Lists can be shared and discussed.

- Have available a variety of shapes pre-cut from construction paper. Invite children to paste the shapes on paper to form a figure. Encourage them to talk about their figure, then write or dictate a caption. Display the captioned shape figures, reading the captions and encouraging the children to read them too.

Fruit Pieces

This hands-on activity lets children learn about the two parts of a whole and the new vocabulary for this pre-math concept, and to create and eat a healthy snack.

What you will need

Apples
Raisins
Knife and cutting board
Tablespoon
Teaspoon
Peanut butter
Bananas

Words you can use

whole	half
fourth	fraction
part	slice
one	two
three	four five
other number words	
apples	bananas
raisins	
other fruit names	
measure	
compare	
size	
amount	
teaspoon	
tablespoon	
other measuring words	

What to do

● Put out apples with peanut butter and raisins or bananas.

● Cut the apples into pieces while the children watch. Depending on the age and abilities of the children they may be able to do this with a dull knife and your assistance.

● Tell the children what you are doing as you perform the action. "I'm cutting the apple in half." Then say, "I'm cutting the apple in _____" and let the children say the word "half." This method of sentence completion lets children to practice new vocabulary.

● Measure the amount of peanut butter you put on each slice of apple with teaspoons and tablespoons. Everyone gets "one teaspoon" or "one tablespoon" of peanut butter. Show the children the difference in the teaspoon and the tablespoon.

● Put the peanut butter on the apple.

● Add raisins and have the children count the raisins as they put them on their apple half.

● Bananas may be used instead of raisins. These should also be counted as they are put on the apple half.

● On other days divide different fruits such as pears, tomatoes, and bananas into halves.

Questions to assess language development

EXPRESSIVE LANGUAGE
....

Can children produce the new words?

RECEPTIVE LANGUAGE
....

Can children pay attention to the new vocabulary?

Literacy Connections

READING EXPERIENCES
....

Eating Fractions by Bruce McMillan

Using food as props, this book introduces the concept of fractions.

Eating the Alphabet: Fruits and Vegetables From A to Z by Lois Ehlert

This book offers beautiful color illustrations of this delicious alphabet.

Give Me Half by Stuart J. Murphy

This simple colorful story reinforces the math concept of halves.

WRITING EXPERIENCES
....

● Have small blank books or food-shaped books for children to draw and write in about their favorite foods.

● Make number charts. On the top of chart paper, write a number. Invite children to find things that have something to do with that number and write the name of the item on the chart. For example, on the "2 Chart," children might write "2 eyes" or "2 hands." Refer to the charts and add to them with new discoveries.

What's Missing?

This activity makes rote counting a fun activity as children try to determine how many items are missing from a group and then try to name the missing items.

What you will need

Scarf

Common objects such as crayon, cup, small ball, spoon, miniature animals, cars or dolls, marker, block, scissors, picture

Words you can use

one

two

three

four

five

other numbers

crayon

cup

small ball

spoon

block

hats

dress-up clothes

miniature animals

cars or dolls

marker

scissors

puppet

book

tambourine

other common objects

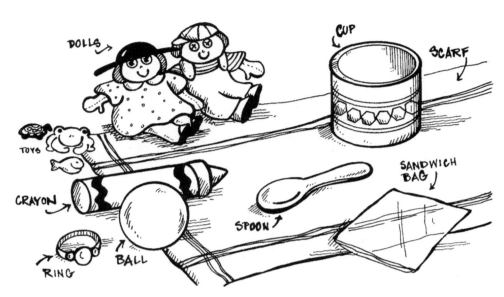

What to do

- Gather a group of common objects that the children would be familiar with. (This activity works best with a small group of children.)
- Put a few of the items (with young children start with just three items) on a table and cover them with a scarf.
- Remove the scarf and ask the children to count the items. After they count them again, cover the items and remove one or more.
- Show the children the remaining items and ask them to count them. They should come up with a different number than the first time.
- After counting the remaining items, prompt the children to name the missing items.
- Continue to increase the number of objects (make sure the number is developmentally appropriate).

Questions to assess language development

EXPRESSIVE LANGUAGE

Can children name the items that are missing from the original count?

RECEPTIVE LANGUAGE

Can the children follow the direction to count?

Do the children know that an item is missing from the original count?

Literacy Connections

READING EXPERIENCES

Five Little Ducks by Raffi

Mother Duck's ducklings leave her one by one, but all come back in the end. Music for this old favorite is presented at the end of the book.

Moon Jump: A Countdown by Paula Brown

In this rhyming subtraction story, cows compete to see which one can jump over the moon. With each failed attempt, readers can join the refrain, "Oh, no! She missed!"

More Than One by Miriam Schlein

One can be two (one pair), seven (one week), nine (one baseball team). What else can one be?

WRITING EXPERIENCES

- Help the children create a "What's Missing Game" by inviting them to write or copy their own names on index cards. Place four or five of these at a time in a line for children to read. Take one away and see if the children can decide which name is missing.

- Invite the children to illustrate a scene from one of the books read with this activity. Encourage them to write or dictate a caption for the illustration. Display drawings and read the captions frequently.

Shop 'til You Drop

The fun and pretend play possibilities in this activity begin to teach math concepts and develop children's vocabulary. Younger children who are not able to count may still understand the idea of exchanging or "buying" things.

What you will need

Tokens
Play money
Pennies
Cash register
Small items for the store
Cigar box or school box
Classroom space for a store

Words you can use

money
token
buy
purchase
more
less
enough
many
few
store
cash register
numerals 1, 2, 3

What to do

- Give each child the same number of tokens.
- Set up a store in an area of the room. Have little toys, stickers, pencils, and erasers set up along a couple of shelves.
- Mark each object with a 1, 2, or 3 as their "price" and put one, two, or three dots on each sticker. For example, a sticker with the numeral 1 will have one dot on it, the sticker with numeral 2 will have two dots, and so on. If appropriate with older children, add more numbers.
- Make a cash register from a cigar box or get a toy cash register.
- Let the children go "shopping" with their tokens. Have them choose what they want.
- Encourage the children to help each other determine if they have enough "money" for the things they have chosen. If necessary, help them count out their tokens at the cash register.

More

Let children take turns being the person who collects the money at the cash register.

Take a field trip to a grocery store. Show children the prices and discuss having enough money for certain items.

Questions to assess language development

Can children say the "price" of items?

Can children rote count their tokens as they pay for items?

Can children formulate sentences to inquire about items they may want to purchase?

RECEPTIVE LANGUAGE

Can children identify the "price tags" on the various items?

Literacy Connections

READING EXPERIENCES

Pigs Will Be Pigs by Amy Axelrod

> The pig family has no money, and they're hungry. They look around for some cash and find enough for four dinners at their favorite restaurant.

Sheep in a Shop by Nancy Shaw

> In another rhyming sheep story, sheep trade their wool for birthday presents.

A Chair for My Mother by Vera Williams

> A young girl, her mother, and grandmother save change in a jar in order to buy a new chair to replace one destroyed in a fire.

Uno, Dos, Tres: 1,2,3 by Pat Mora

> Two sisters go from shop to shop to buy birthday presents for their mother. Numbers from one to ten are presented in both English and Spanish.

WRITING EXPERIENCES

- Encourage children to write shopping lists before trading in their tokens.
- Have a variety of literacy materials available at the dramatic play center. Include receipts, order pads, sticky pads for price tags, and so on. While playing in the center, model how to use the materials and encourage children to use them.

So Big

Encourage children to practice pre-math skills by measuring themselves from their heads to their feet. They fill in the blank with words for units of measurement with the phrase "I am _____."

What you will need

Tape measure
Scale
Yardstick
Large paper
Colored markers

Words you can use

weight
weigh
pounds
height
feet
inches
yardstick
measure
measurement
measuring tape
scale
head
toe
length
chart
record
around (circumference)

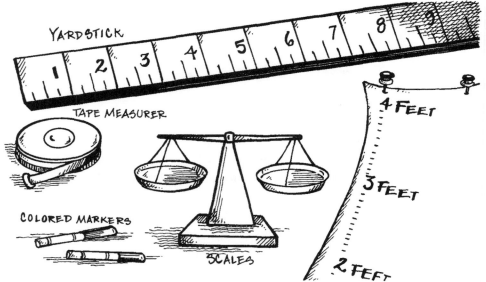

What to do

- Show the children the tools to measure themselves. A yardstick or measuring tape and a scale will work.
- Measure around each child's head and waist with a tape measure. Record the measurements.
- Measure each child's feet with a tape measure taped to the ground. Record the measurements.
- Weigh each child. Record the measurements.
- Display the chart.
- Update the chart periodically throughout the year.

Questions to assess language development

EXPRESSIVE LANGUAGE

Can children name (label) the tools used for measurement?
Can children formulate sentences to respond to about measurement?

Can children identify the tools used for measurement?

Can children identify the numbers on the measuring tools?

Literacy Connections

READING EXPERIENCES

The Story of Imelda, Who Was Small by Lurie Morris

Imelda is so small she sleeps in a shoe box. The doctor tells her to eat long foods like spaghetti if she wants to grow tall.

The Best Bug Parade by Stuart Murphy

This simple book introduces the math concept of size comparison using bugs.

Inch by Inch by Leo Lionni

A clever inchworm talks a robin out of eating him by measuring and counting the inches until he is out of sight of the robin.

WRITING EXPERIENCES

- Invite children to make charts or books titled "Bigger Than Me" and "Smaller Than Me." Encourage them to draw, write, or dictate things that fit on the appropriate chart.

- Have children write their names on index cards. Help them line their names in order from tallest to shortest, heaviest to lightest, and so on.

Higher and Higher

Children determine their height using non-standard units of measurement. The language of measurement may be new for some children, so these words should be modeled and explained as the children interact with the measuring material.

What you will need

Blocks
Masking tape
Graph paper
Crayons
Poster board for class graph

Words you can use

tall
high
height
measure
head to toe
discover
graph
how many
stack
line
long
number names

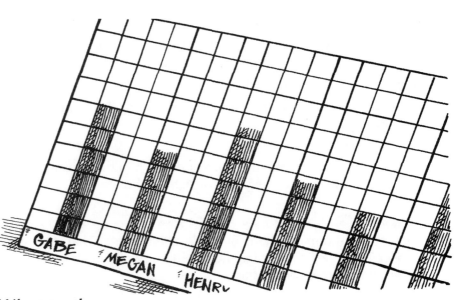

What to do

● Ask the children, "How many blocks high (big) are you?" and "How can we find out?"

● Let the children work out the process for measuring each other. They might lie on the floor and place the blocks from head to toe or they might stack the blocks to reach the measured child's height. Let the children discover for themselves a method that will provide them with the answer.

● Give each child a piece of graph paper. Have them color in the appropriate number of blocks to represent their individual heights.

● Make a class block graph chart that has a column of blocks above each child's name. When the children learn their individual block height they can color in the correct number of blocks. (See illustration.)

More

Use other types of non-standard measuring devices. Ask the children, "What else might we use to measure how tall we are?" (Answers might be string, yarn sticks, and rocks.)

Have the children measure other items in the room.

Questions to assess language development

Can children rote count using their nonstandard unit of measurement?

Can children say "how big" they are?

RECEPTIVE LANGUAGE

Can children respond to various forms of "How tall (big, high) are you?"

Literacy Connections

READING EXPERIENCES

George Shrinks by William Joyce

> When George's dream of becoming small comes true, he has to do all his daily chores with giant tools.

Just a Little Bit by Ann Tompert

> Elephant is sitting on one end of the seesaw with Mouse, Giraffe, Zebra, Lion, Bear, Crocodile, Mongoose, Monkey, and Ostrich on the other end. They can't seem to get Elephant's side off the ground. How will they ever be able to balance out?

The Line-up Book by Marisabina Russo

> Sam lines up everything in his bedroom, including himself, in order to reach the kitchen in one line.

Tiny for a Day by Dick Gackenbach

> Sidney invents a way to shrink things, including himself.

WRITING EXPERIENCES

- Have small blank books or chart paper available with titles such as "Bigger Than Me," and "Smaller than Me." Invite children to draw, write, or dictate things that would be appropriate for each title.

- Help children create webs of big and little things. In the center of a piece of chart paper write the word *big*. As children name big things, write their words around the center word. Do the same thing for *little*. Other size words can be used, such as *heavy* and *light*.

- Encourage children to make small books to record the different ways they measured themselves. For example, on one page they may write or dictate "I am 7 blocks tall." Another may say, "My feet are 10 Legos long."

Cubby Counting

The cubby area is a perfect place to reinforce number concepts and to practice rote counting and sorting. Children learn number words and categorizing skills.

What you will need

Storage area with containers of familiar items

Cubby area

Words you can use

one	two
three	four
five	
other number names	
hat	coat
gloves	sweater
scarf	boots
shoes	socks
pants	shirts
belt	
other clothing names	
count	
how many	

What to do

- Go to the cubby area or storage area where various items are kept.
- Ask the children to pick an item such as a hat, coat, and gloves and count how many of that item they can find in the cubbies.

More

Encourage additional counting in the classroom. How many plates, glasses, cups are on the snack table? How many chairs are in this room? How many buttons on your shirt, coat, or dress?

Count kitchen utensils (forks, spoons) in the dramatic play area, and ice cubes in a glass during snack. Children might also predict how many ice cubes they think might fill drinking glasses of varying sizes.

Count blocks in a container.

Questions to assess language development

EXPRESSIVE LANGUAGE

Can children count out loud?

Can children follow as you count items?

Literacy Connections

READING EXPERIENCES

One, Two, One Pair! by Bruce McMillan

> Using real photos, readers can count things that come in pairs, such as socks, feet, gloves, and so on. Even the child in the photos turns out to be one of a pair—of twins.

Ten Cats Have Hats: A Counting Book by Jean Marzollo

> The child in this rhyming story gets a new hat on each page.

This Old Man by Carol Jones

> In this version of the familiar counting song, a young girl and her grandfather do things together such as gather eggs, have a cookout, and take care of the bees.

WRITING EXPERIENCES

● Have small blank books available for children to record amounts as they count things in their cubbies. With a title such as, "What's In Tommy's Cubby?" children can draw, write, or dictate things from their own cubby.

● Make graphs of things counted. For example, one graph might record the number of clothing items found such as hats and gloves. Another graph might be used to record the number of school items, such as paints or boxes of crayons.

● Encourage children to make signs for things they count. For example, they could write "5 paint jars" or "6 hats." Hang the signs near the items counted and refer to them when putting things away.

Counting My Toes

This activity focuses on parts of the body, a subject that young children are comfortable and familiar with. It allows them to build math skills while talking about something familiar to them. This activity can take place over a number of sequential days.

What you will need

Just curiosity

Words you can use

head	neck
eyes	nose
mouth	lips
tongue	teeth
fingers	ears
hands	feet
legs	knees
ankles	arms
other parts of the body	
one	two
three	four
five	
other numbers	

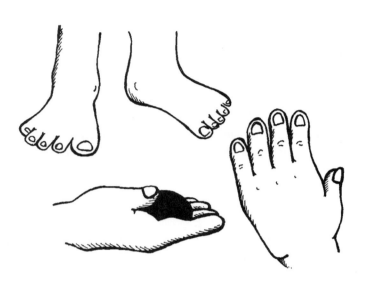

What to do

- Tell the children that everyone is going to count the parts of their bodies. Ask them to point to their ears, their hands, their fingers, their eyes, and their noses. Encourage them to take off one shoe and sock and point to their toes.
- Count each part of the body in unison.
- Start at the head. Count eyes, nose, ears, lips, tongues, and teeth.
- Continue to the limbs. Count arms, elbows, wrists, shoulders, hands, fingers, fingernails, and thumbs.
- Count belly buttons, legs, knees, ankles, and feet.
- Finish with toes.
- Adjust the counting according to the ages and abilities of the children. Keep it enjoyable and somewhat novel for the children.

More

Encourage the children to draw stick people. As the children count each body part, have them draw it on their stick people. Display their finished drawings after all parts of the body are counted.

Go around to each child and count something that the child is wearing. For example, count two sleeves on Suzie's shirt and five buttons on Joe's.

Questions to assess language development

EXPRESSIVE LANGUAGE

Can children name (label) parts of the body?

Can children count various parts of the body?

RECEPTIVE LANGUAGE

Can children identify parts of the body?

Literacy Connections

READING EXPERIENCES

I Spy Two Eyes by Lucy Micklethwait

This book is part of the *Eye Spy* series.

Let's Count It Out, Jesse Bear by Nancy White Carlstrom

In this counting book, everyone's favorite bear is on a trip to an amusement park and does lots of funny things that require counting.

WRITING EXPERIENCES

- Have small blank books available with numbers as titles. Talk about which body parts would fit in each book such as one nose in the "One" book or two eyes in the "Two" book. Invite children to draw, write, or dictate about the body parts in the appropriate books.

- Make charts to record the number of different body parts.

- Place a photo or drawing of a body in the middle of chart paper. Help children name different body parts. Label each.

Number Hunt

How many things are labeled with numbers? Look around and you may be surprised. Then name (label) these items to boost children's expressive vocabulary.

What you will need

Post-it notes

Words you can use

watch
clock
calendar
telephone
computer
book
toys
discover
numbers
find
how many
search
look
observe
hunt
names of items found

What to do

- Encourage the children to walk around the room. Ask them to look closely at everything in the room to see if they can find something that has a number or numbers on it.
- As the children find items, they should mark them with Post-it notes. They might discover numbers on a clock, a watch, a calendar, a box, a telephone, a computer, a printer, and a book.
- This activity might cover a period of days as the children continue to discover numbered items on toys, tables, and other items.
- Count the stickers daily, make note of the numbers on items, and remind the children to keep searching.

More

Take the children on an outdoor number hunt. They will find many more numbered items such as license plates and mailboxes.

Questions to assess language development

EXPRESSIVE LANGUAGE

Can children name (label) the items on which they find the numbers?

RECEPTIVE LANGUAGE

Can children identify numbers on items?

Literacy Connections

READING EXPERIENCES

How Many, How Many, How Many by Rick Walton

> Each page is a rhymed counting riddle about familiar sets, such as the number of fingers, months, and so on.

Ten Black Dots by Donald Crews

> Simple black dots become a variety of things in this simple rhyming counting book.

More Than One by Miriam Schlein

> One can be two (one pair), seven (one week), nine (one baseball team). What else can one be?

WRITING EXPERIENCES

- On charts or in individual books, help children write or dictate their own number rhymes about such common things as shoes on their feet and eggs in a carton.

- Encourage children to "inventory" the food in the dramatic play center. Help children count and record how many vegetables, fruits, and other items are in the refrigerator or on the shelf. Or, they may want to record how many green foods, red foods, and brown foods are in the center.

The M&M Challenge

Many children enjoy the "melt in your mouth, not in your hand" candy. Why not use this treat as an activity to stimulate language development, develop the math skills of sorting and counting, and encourages color recognition?

What you will need

Napkins
Mini-size M&M candies
Spoon

Words you can use

package
how many
different
pile
number
group
candy
count
sort
graph
name
amount
round
circle
red
blue
yellow
brown
green
other color names

What to do

- Spoon some mini-size M&M's onto a napkin for each child.
- The children look at all the different colors and try to name them. Assist the children in naming the colors if necessary.
- Encourage the children to sort their M&M's by color. They may choose to do this in a separate pile or in a line graph for each color.
- Compare the various colors and the amounts of each.
- After the activity is completed, the children can eat their M&M's.

More

Look around the room and find items that have the same colors as the M&M's.

Also look for items that have the same round shape.

What color is the most prevalent in the room?

Do the same for the children's clothing.

Questions to assess language development

Can children name (label) the colors of the M&M's?

Can children rote count the M&M's as they are sorted?

RECEPTIVE LANGUAGE

Can children identify colors of the M&M's?

Literacy Connections

READING EXPERIENCES

Every Buddy Counts by Stuart J. Murphy
   Children will enjoy counting the buddies from one little hamster to ten cuddly teddy bears.

Hippos Go Berserk by Sandra Boynton
   This funny counting book with 45 hippos and a mystery creature makes counting an adventure.

The M&M's Brand Chocolate Candies Counting Book by Barbara McGrath
   This colorful book will make counting M&M's lots of fun!

WRITING EXPERIENCES

● Have small blank books available with the title "My Color Book" and the name of a different color on each page. Invite the children to write and draw in their book using crayons or markers that match the color word on each page. You may want to write their words for them. Encourage children to take their books home to read to their families.

● Make M&M color charts. On a piece of chart paper write the word "Red." Let each child tell how many M&M's of that color they had. Write their words on the chart, such as "Nancy had five red M&M's" or "Mark had more red ones than green ones."

Trail Mix Math

A simple trail mix has numerous ingredients that can be both sorted and counted to learn math concepts, such as more or less. The graphing step emphasizes emerging literacy in addition to exposing the children to a practical math and science skill.

What you will need

Ingredients for trail mix, large serving bowl (plastic), and large wooden spoon

or

Purchased trail mix

Measuring cup

Paper plates or bowls

Words you can use

mix	stir
peanuts	pecans
walnuts	almonds
other nut names	
sort	count
numbers	more
less	trail mix
snack	energy
orange	apple
banana	grapes
other fruit names	
pumpkin seeds, sunflower seeds	
other seed names	

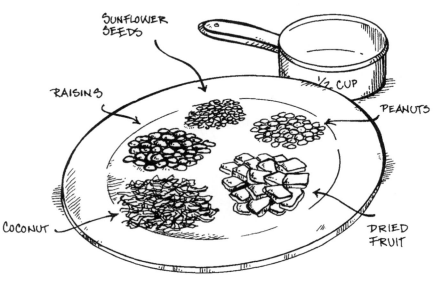

SUNFLOWER SEEDS

RAISINS

½ CUP

PEANUTS

COCONUT

DRIED FRUIT

What to do

● With the children, prepare this snack from scratch (see recipe below) or use purchased trail mix.

● Let the children pour and mix the various ingredients into a large serving bowl.

● The children stir the ingredients and mix them thoroughly.

● Give each child a turn to pour about one cup (250 ml) of the mix onto a paper plate for snack.

● The children can sort and count the raisins, nuts, and dried fruit pieces. They can also count how many they have of each ingredient as they eat the mix.

● Put leftovers in a plastic bag for the children to take home.

Note: As with any food or cooking activity, wash hands before handing food and check for any food allergies.

TRAIL MIX RECIPE   (MAKES THREE QUARTS)

2 cups (500 ml) pumpkin seeds

1 cup (250 ml) sunflower seeds

½ cup (125 ml) pecans

½ cup (125 ml) shredded coconut

2 cups (500 ml) raisins

1 cup (250 ml) peanuts

½ cup (125 ml) almonds

Place all ingredients into a bowl and mix thoroughly.

More

Make a picture recipe of the steps the children are to follow as they prepare the mix.

Each child can make a "Trail Mix" graph.

Make a graph for the entire class.

Questions to assess language development

EXPRESSIVE LANGUAGE

Can children rote count items in the food groups?

Can children name (label) the ingredients in the trail mix?

RECEPTIVE LANGUAGE

Can children follow directions from recipe pictures and oral descriptions?

Can children sort the various items used to make the trail mix?

Literacy Connections

READING EXPERIENCES

- Have a variety of simple recipes (such as those in *Cup Cooking* by
  Barbara Johnson and Betty Plemons) available to refer to for cooking
  experiences.

- Place cookbooks in the dramatic play center for children to use in
  their play.

WRITING EXPERIENCES

- Invite children to decide on the ingredients for a Number Salad; for
  example, one banana, two apples, three oranges. Write their recipe
  on a chart. Refer to the chart while helping the children make the
  salad.

First, Second, Finally

Children at the developing language stage are beginning to understand time and sequence. This activity promotes the use of terms such as first, second, and last in stories that have a sequential action.

What you will need

Story

Art materials

Words you can use

first

second

third

next

last

finally

in the end

yesterday

today

tomorrow

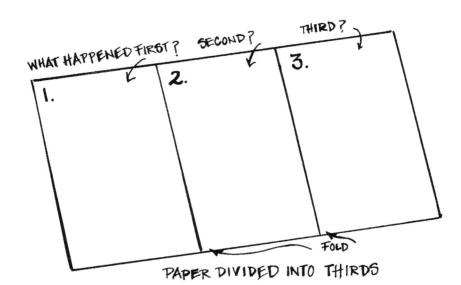

PAPER DIVIDED INTO THIRDS

What to do

● Choose a favorite story with sequential actions to work with (fairy tales and folktales are good examples). Read it to the children.

● Have the children act out the story. Talk about what happens first, what happens in the middle, and what happens in the end.

● Divide the story into three parts so that it is less complicated. For example, Goldilocks went for a walk to her grandmother's house. When she got there the wolf was dressed up like her grandmother to trick her. He chased her around until the woodsman killed him.

● Encourage each child to make a storyboard. Give them a long piece of paper divided into three pieces. The first section is What Happened First?, the second section is What Happened Next?, and the third is What Happened Last? Encourage them to draw pictures for each section.

● Display the children's drawings. Have them retell the story later on in the day.

More

Have the children act out the three different parts of the story.

Choose a story with things that happened in the past, present, and future.

Talk to the children about things you did yesterday, things you will do today, and things you will do tomorrow.

Questions to assess language development

EXPRESSIVE LANGUAGE

Can children act out a story in a three-part sequence?

RECEPTIVE LANGUAGE

Can children follow a sequence of first, second, last?

Literacy Connections

READING EXPERIENCES

● Read other stories. Photocopy three or four illustrations from different parts of the book. Use a flannel board or glue the illustrations to tongue depressors and help children retell the story while placing the illustrations in correct order.

WRITING EXPERIENCES

● Invite children to record the things they do throughout the day in a daily journal where they can draw, write, or dictate events.

● As a regular daily routine, plan a review time for the end of the day. As you discuss the things the children did, record the events in order. Keep the chart up and refer to it the next day to remind the children of the things they have done.

Number People

This activity makes children aware of numbers. The auditory portion of the activity, listening for the cue word during the day, allows children to enjoy the number names.
Note: This is an advanced activity.

What you will need

10 original number people
Drawings of each
10 original rhymes

Words you can use

one
two
three
four
five
other number words
first
second
third
only
few
more
some
any
other quantity words

What to do

● Make Number People. Give your number people a corresponding numbers of buttons, hairs, fingers, toes, eyes, or teeth. Mr. Number 1 can have one leg to stand on, Mr. Number 2 can have two eyes to see with, Ms. Number 3 can have three teeth to chew with, and Mrs. Number 4 can have four toes to stand with. Be creative and have fun making up your number people.

● Make simple drawings of each number person, from one to ten. Have each drawing take up a page.

● Start at the beginning of a month. At circle time (or any other time during the day) on the first day of the month, teach about Mr. Number 1. Show the children a calendar and say, "Today is the first day of the month. Today we are going to meet Mr. Number 1."

● Throughout the day, stress quantity words that relate to the number you are working on. For example, first, only, single, alone. Every time something comes up that allows you to stress the word or concept of one, take advantage of it. Say, "Suzie, you just put *only one* block in the container!" Encourage the children to name the item also.

● Make up a rhyme about Mr. Number 1. For example, "Mr. Number 1, he is a lot of fun! He likes to shake his leg and dance in the sun!" It doesn't have to make a lot of sense. The sillier it is, the more the children will love it!

- Try to make up rhymes that the children can act out. In the example given above, the children can learn the rhyme and then stand up and hop on one leg while singing it.
- Count throughout the day. Everything you pick up say, "ONE crayon! ONE block! ONE doll!"
- On the next day, the second day of the new month, do the same with Mr. Number 2. Continue until you have learned all ten Number people.

More

Have the children help you make up the rhymes about the number people. Put the rhyme to a familiar melody and sing it all day.

Questions to assess language development

EXPRESSIVE LANGUAGE

Can children use the number words?

Can children use the words related to various numbers?

RECEPTIVE LANGUAGE

Can children identify one item as illustrated by Mr. Number 1?

Literacy Connections

READING EXPERIENCES

Count! by Denise Fleming

Animals from 1 to 10 bounce, crawl, and jump across the page.

Big Fat Hen by Keith Baker

A new interpretation of a familiar rhyme invites readers to count hatching chicks, buzzing bees, and other animals.

One Red Rooster by Kathleen Sullivan Carroll

Readers rhyme and count farm animals from one red rooster to ten sleeping pigs.

What Comes in Twos, Threes and Fours? by Suzanne Aker

This book uses familiar things to help build the concepts of two, three, and four.

WRITING EXPERIENCES

- Take photos or find magazine pictures of familiar and not-so-familiar items. Glue pictures to large pieces of chart paper. Invite children to count and name (label) things in the pictures, such as two airplane wings, three tricycle wheels, and so on. Put the pages into a big book to be shared and place in the library corner.

Science

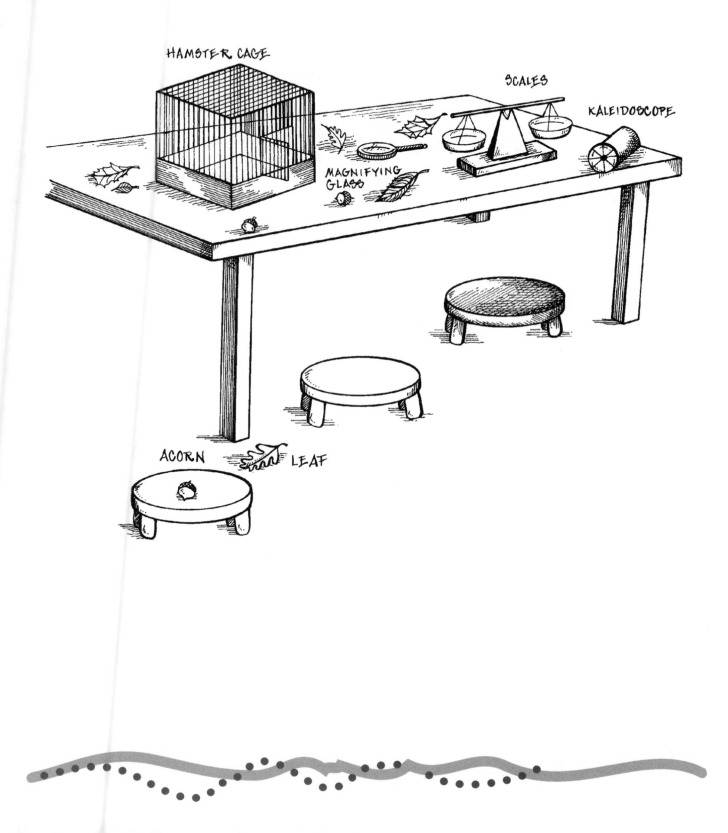

HAMSTER CAGE

SCALES

KALEIDOSCOPE

MAGNIFYING GLASS

ACORN   LEAF

Animal Homes

Every living thing has a home of some kind. This activity allows children to use new vocabulary pertaining to animals, insects, and their homes. Correct use of such pronouns as *they, I, he, she,* and *my* can be highlighted as this is an emerging skill for preschoolers.

What you will need

Books about different animal
    homes
Paper
Crayons

Words you can use

hot
desert
sea
rain forest
ocean
mountains
home
frozen
house
North Pole
animal names
he, she, they, it
I, my, mine, me

What to do

- Choose two different animals or insects with very different homes. Try to find a book that tells about each animal and its natural habitat. The animals could be male or female in the stories. Read the books with the children.

- After reading of the books, have the children draw each animal in its home. Discuss what *he* would eat or what *she* looks like. Talk about the differences and similarities between the two animal homes.

- Invite the children to talk about their own homes and what they like to eat, drink, wear, etc. A difference/likeness discussion can follow, during which the personal pronouns *I, me, my, mine,* and so on can be highlighted.

Questions to assess language development

EXPRESSIVE LANGUAGE

Can children name a variety of animals?

Can children name a variety of homes lived in by animals?

RECEPTIVE LANGUAGE

Can children identify a wide variety of animals?

Can children associate the appropriate homes with various animals?

Literacy Connections

READING EXPERIENCES

Any Room for Me? by Loek Koopmans

> A woodcutter drops his mitten in the forest and it becomes a warm home for a mouse and other animals.

A House is a House for Me by Mary Ann Hoberman

> Children will learn about dwellings in this rhyme book that tells them, "A hill is a house for an ant, an ant. A hive is a house for a bee."

Is This a House for Hermit Crab? by Megan McDonald

> Hermit Crab is looking for a new home, but he doesn't find it until a wave carries him out to sea.

Where do Bears Sleep? by Barbara Shook Hazen

> This gentle book shows how and where various animals settle down to sleep.

WRITING EXPERIENCES

- Record the children's discussions about the differences and similarities between animal homes on chart paper. Read the words aloud.

- Invite children to illustrate an animal's home. Encourage them to write or dictate a caption for their illustrations. Compile the pages into a book.

- Have small blank books available for children to create their own books about animal homes.

Behind the Wall

Barrier games have long been a source of practice opportunity for expressive language skills. Children utilize descriptive words to describe an invisible item to other children, while the listeners attempt to guess what the child is describing. Asking questions is a skill that can be practiced here. Basic descriptive vocabulary is emphasized in a fun activity. Remember, "no peeking."

What you will need

Common objects
Pictures of common objects
Barrier

Words you can use

big
little
tiny
soft
rough
hard
smooth
color words
function words
shape words
"Is it . . ."

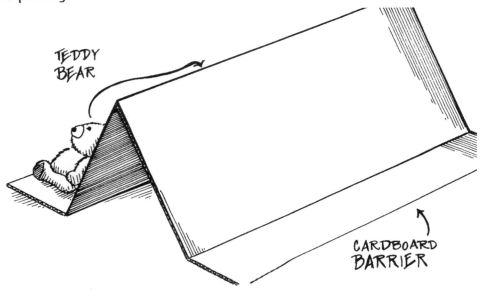

TEDDY BEAR

CARDBOARD BARRIER

What to do

● Have the children practice descriptive words that might apply to objects, such as size, shape, color, and usage. Let them know they will be using these types of words in a game.

● Construct a "barrier" between two children, or between a child and a group. A book set on end or a short room divider will work.

● Have the child behind the barrier choose a familiar, common object to describe. Use real objects first, then move to pictures of common objects. Remind the child to use descriptive words, NOT the name of the object.

● The child or group that cannot see the object tries to guess what it is from the descriptive words. At first, you may need to prompt the children to ask the necessary questions.

● Give other children the opportunity to describe an object behind the barrier.

More

When children advance to the level where they can utilize pictures, emphasize one particular category such as animals, articles of clothing, and forms of transportation.

Questions to assess language development

EXPRESSIVE LANGUAGE

Can children tell something "about" an item without telling the name of
   the item?

Can children formulate questions to get more needed information about
   items?

RECEPTIVE LANGUAGE

Can children guess the item by listening to descriptors?

Literacy Connections

READING EXPERIENCES

Mac and Marie and the Train Toss Surprise by Elizabeth Howard

   Two children try to guess what's in a package that their uncle has
   promised to toss from a train. Listeners can guess, too.

Once There was a Bull...(Frog) by Rick Walton

   Help Frog find his lost "hop" with this engaging guessing game, and
   look for the surprise on each page.

Peck, Slither, and Slide by Suse MacDonald

   A fun guessing game reinforces vocabulary by giving a verb on one
   page and the animal it describes on the next.

What Am I? Looking Through Shapes at Apples and Grapes by N.N.
   Charles

   Invite children to guess which fruit grows behind each die-cut shape.

WRITING EXPERIENCES

● Take photos of familiar and unfamiliar objects. Glue each photo to a
   large piece of chart paper. Write the words on the paper that the
   children use to describe the object. Read the words together when
   finished. Display the charts and refer to them occasionally.

● Have small blank books available with titles such as "Small and Furry"
   and "Round and Rough." Invite children to draw illustrations for the
   books, writing or dictating captions.

● Have small blank books cut in shapes such as circles and triangles.
   Invite children to draw and write about objects that have the same
   shape as the book.

Touch and Tell

Children utilize their sense of touch as they explore their environment. Information received through the tactile sense can help children to develop language concepts. Labeling items by feel can assist children in integrating various sensory inputs.

What you will need

Familiar items such as plastic fruit, small cars, trucks, animals, cups, plates, and paint-brushes

Unfamiliar items

Words you can use

touch
big
blindfold
feel
little
vision
soft
rough
hard
smooth
sharp
round

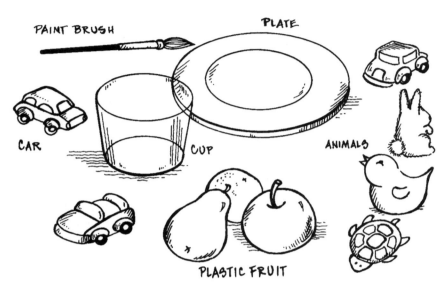

PAINT BRUSH   PLATE   CAR   CUP   ANIMALS   PLASTIC FRUIT

What to do

● Gather a small group of children. Blindfold one child and hand her a familiar object from a group she has previously seen displayed.

● The blindfolded child tells the other children what kind of item she is feeling using descriptive words such as soft, hard, big, little, rough, and smooth.

● The child removes the blindfold to see what the item is.

More

Provide items that are familiar but have not been previously displayed.

Provide items that are not familiar.

Questions to assess language development

EXPRESSIVE LANGUAGE

Can children label familiar items as they are displayed?

Can children label familiar items by feel?

Can children use descriptive terms to tell about the item they are feeling but not seeing?

Literacy Connections

READING EXPERIENCES

I Can Tell By Touching by Carolyn Otto

A boy shares how he knows his own world through the sense of touch. Includes a simple experiment for children to compare the sensitivity of our hands to the rest of our skin.

Night Sounds, Morning Colors by Rosemary Wells

Beautiful language and illustrations make the sounds of night and colors of morning come alive.

Sense Suspense: A Guessing Game for the Five Senses by Bruce McMillan

Two children in Puerto Rico share the sights of their island. The reader is asked to use the color photos to guess what each object is, and then tell which senses they would use to experience it.

WRITING EXPERIENCES

- Take a photo of each object used during this activity. Glue a photo to a large piece of chart paper. Write the words on the paper that the children use to describe the object. Read the words together when finished. Display the charts and refer to them occasionally.

- Have small blank books available with titles such as "Small and Furry" or "Round and Rough." Invite children to draw illustrations for the books and write or dictate captions.

How Does It Feel

The world is full of materials that have different textures. Using the sense of touch, children use descriptive words that tell about the textures they feel.

What you will need

Items that have different textures such as acorns, rocks, leaves, grass, pine needles, glass, plastic, fabric swatches, sandpaper

Words you can use

touch

texture

feel

smooth

hard

soft

rough

slippery

same

different

bumpy

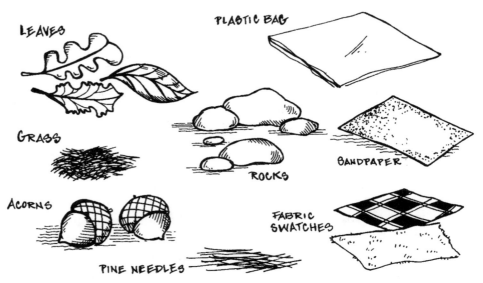

What to do

- Show the children objects that have different textures such as acorns, glass, wood, sandpaper, paper, and plastic. As they touch the object, ask them how it feels. Introduce texture words as they touch. Is it rough, smooth, soft, hard, bumpy, etc.?

- Take the children on a texture walk. Examine and touch rocks, twigs, leaves, pine cones, pine needles, grass, soil, acorns, bark, nuts, and other available items.

- As the children examine an object, ask them to describe how it feels.

More

Follow the same procedure using swatches of fabric, wallpaper samples, and a variety of rocks.

On the walk, examine trees only.

Questions to assess language development

EXPRESSIVE LANGUAGE

Can children say descriptive words to tell about various objects?

RECEPTIVE LANGUAGE

Can children find textures, such as smooth, as you name them?

Literacy Connections

READING EXPERIENCES

Fuzzy Yellow Ducklings by Matthew Van Fleet

> Everyone will enjoy this touch-and-feel book with its textures, shapes, colors, and animals.

The Very Busy Spider by Eric Carl

> Spider spins a web that can be felt as well as seen on every page.

Windsongs and Rainbows by Albert Burton

> This great read-aloud contains delightful descriptions of the wind, the rain, the sun, and the storm as experienced by the senses.

WRITING EXPERIENCES

- Invite children to sort objects by their textures. Encourage them to write or dictate labels for their groups such as "Smooth Rocks," or "Fuzzy Leaves." Have them display their labels and groupings for others to see.

- During the texture walk, invite children to take along clipboards and to write down the names of things they find that match a particular texture. After the walk, they can share what they observed while you write their words on a chart.

- Using wallpaper samples as covers for small blank books, invite children to draw, write, or dictate names of things that have a texture similar to the wallpaper cover. For example, if you used flocked wallpaper for the cover, children could describe fuzzy things and if you used textured wallpaper, they could describe bumpy things.

Weight Time

Children discover the concept of weight early in their development. This is especially true when they are trying to lift something that they can't budge. This science opportunity gives the children plenty of opportunities to talk about weight in an environment that they can control.

What you will need

Balance scale

Rocks of various weights and sizes

Words you can use

weigh

compare

scale

balance

rocks

heavy

heavier

heaviest

light

lighter

lightest

small

smaller

smallest

big

bigger

biggest

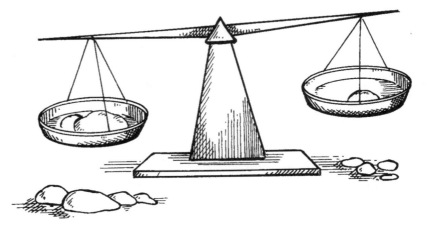

What to do

- Show the children how to use a balance scale.
- Give the children an assortment of rocks of various sizes.
- Ask the children which rock is the heaviest and which rock is the lightest. Tell them that they can find out by weighting them. Let them put one rock in each of the two balance pans on the scale.
- Let the children weigh all of the rocks, comparing the heaviest to the lightest.

More

Place the rocks in a line with the heaviest first and the lightest last.

Give the children other items to compare weights such as acorns and twigs.

See if they can balance the rocks on the scale.

Questions to assess language development

Can children say the weight and size terms?

RECEPTIVE LANGUAGE

Can children identify the rocks you describe with words like small, smaller, smallest?

Do children understand the comparative (smaller) and superlative (smallest) forms?

Literacy Connections

READING EXPERIENCES

Everybody Needs a Rock by Byrd Baylor

This book helps children appreciate the variety and wonder of rocks.

The Mouse and the Potato by Thomas Berger and Carla Grillis

The farmer's daughter plants a big potato that grows into such a large plant that it takes the whole farmer's family—the dog, the cat, and the mouse—to pull it out of the ground.

WRITING EXPERIENCES

- Invite children to make charts or books titled "Bigger Than Me" and "Smaller Than Me." Encourage them to draw, write, or dictate things that fit on the appropriate chart or in the appropriate book.

- Have children write their names on index cards. Help them line up their names in order from tallest to shortest.

- Have small blank books or chart paper available with titles such as "Heavier Than Me" and "Lighter than Me." Invite children to draw, write, or dictate things that would be appropriate for each title.

- Help children create webs of big and little things. In the center of a piece of chart paper write the word "heavy." As children name heavy things, write their words around the center word. Do the same thing for "light."

Space Mud

Making goop is a tried-and-true activity that children can enjoy as they explore and discover various forms of matter. This activity will emphasize the sequential directions for the creation of goop. Try this new recipe and enjoy the descriptive language that is sure to follow.

What you will need

White glue
Water
Borax
Food coloring (optional)

Words you can use

feel
touch
cold
wet
icky
shape
color
change
soft
gooey

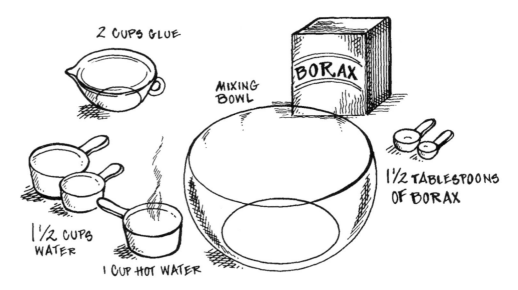

2 CUPS GLUE

BORAX

MIXING BOWL

1½ TABLESPOONS OF BORAX

1½ CUPS WATER

1 CUP HOT WATER

What to do

- Prepare the recipe (see page 245) with the children (if closely supervised) or ahead of time.
- Observe the mixture as it forms a suspension. Allow the mixture to cool.
- Give each child a glob of the Space Mud and let them interact with it.
- You will not have to ask them how it feels. They will tell you!
- Give them ample time to play with the mud.

More

Add food coloring to reinforce primary color concepts.

Questions to assess language development

EXPRESSIVE LANGUAGE

Can children tell you what the "space mud" feels like, smells like, moves like?

Can children follow directions as the "space mud" is created?

Literacy Connections

READING EXPERIENCES

Bartholomew and the Oobleck by Dr. Seuss

Kind Derwin's magicians create a new type of sticky weather that confuses the whole kingdom.

Clay Boy by Mirra Ginsberg

In this Russian folktale, a greedy clay boy tries to eat everyone and everything in his small village until he runs into a young goat.

Mud Pies and Other Recipes: A Cookbook for Dolls by Marjorie Winslow

This book, a wonderful collection of recipes for a doll tea party, makes playing with mud even more fun.

WRITING EXPERIENCES

● When weather permits, allow the children to go outside and write with mud and sticks on the playground or walk.

● Invite children to dictate their recipes for mud pies. Collect the recipes in a book for reading to the class. Place the book in the class library or in the dramatic play center.

● Make a chart of sticky or gooey words and muddy things. Encourage children to give words to add to the chart. Show how you can refer back to books you've read to find descriptive words like these.

SPACE MUD RECIPE

2 cups glue

1½ cups room-temperature water

1 cup hot water

1½ level tablespoons Borax

Combine glue and water, and blend thoroughly. Add food coloring if desired. In large bowl combine hot water and borax, stirring until borax is completely dissolved. Slowly pour glue mixture into borax mixture, stirring constantly. (Recipe from Barnes Jewish Day Care, St. Louis, MO.)

Pollution Solution

Our world is being littered, polluted, and spoiled! If we all pitch in we can make a difference. This activity helps the children to become aware of the problem and to talk, utilizing new and appropriate vocabulary, about some ways that they can help to prevent pollution.

What you will need

Chewing gum or candy bar
   wrapper

Words you can use

trash

garbage

pollution

throw away

pretend

picnic

soda

lunch

litter

litter bug

dirty

ground

water

car

TRASH →

BANANA PEEL

What to do

● Ask the children if they know what a litterbug is. Have they ever seen one? Explain that a litterbug is a person who throws trash on the ground or in the water instead of in the trash can.

● Take a plastic wrapper from your pocket and throw it on the floor and walk away from it. Ask the children to respond to the action that they just saw.

● Ask the children if they think you are a litterbug and what you should have done with the trash on the floor.

● Ask the children if they have seen people throw things on the floor, on the ground, or in the water that they shouldn't. Do they think these people are litterbugs?

● Talk about the following situations with the children to create awareness and action to stop littering.

   ✓ You are eating a banana in the car on the way to grandmother's house. Where are you going to put the peel?

   ✓ You have finished drinking a soda. Where are you going to put the can?

   ✓ You are on a picnic with your family near a beautiful lake. After lunch you see that there isn't a trash can nearby. What are you going to do with your garbage?

- Let the children suggest other scenarios where they might have the opportunity to litter and what they might do to prevent it.

- Act out a picnic. Pretend to go to the lake in a car and have a picnic. Pass out make-believe food such as potato chips, apples, and sandwiches and enjoy your "lunch." When it's time to go home, look around and see that there is no trash can. Ask the children what they think you should do with your (pretend) trash. Pass around a (pretend) bag and ask the children to put their trash into it. Point out that the lake is still a beautiful place because no litter is left behind.

More

Children take a walk around the block and collect trash. When they return to the center they can make a trash collage.

Literacy Connections

READING EXPERIENCES

Dinosaurs to the Rescue! A Guide to Protecting Our Planet by Laurene Krasny Brown and Marc Brown

The dinosaurs in this book discover ways to conserve and recycle and show readers simple ways to take care of the earth.

Prince William by Gloria Rand

Denny finds an oil-coated baby seal after a tanker hits a reef and spills its cargo into Alaska's Prince William Sound. Denny names her seal Prince William and takes it to a rescue center, where it is saved.

Someday a Tree by Eve Bunting

Alice's special tree is dying because someone dumped poisonous chemicals near it.

WRITING EXPERIENCES

- Put recycled paper in the writing center and encourage children to write on the back.

- Help children draw, write, or dictate signs and labels encouraging others to recycle. Post them near trash cans around the building. Be sure to use recycled paper.

- Take a walk around the school yard, looking for signs of pollution. Invite children to list their observations on clipboards. Then compile their lists on a class chart.

Questions to assess language development

EXPRESSIVE LANGUAGE

Can children label "littering" in various settings?

Can children label items that may be seen as pollution?

RECEPTIVE LANGUAGE

Can children identify "littering" as it occurs?

Kaleidoscope

Making kaleidoscopes from simple materials can help children to sequence steps in a creative endeavor. Children can then use the kaleidoscopes creatively to describe what they see.

What you will need

Toilet paper tubes
Tape
Scissors
White tissue paper
Colored felt-tip markers

Words you can use

pretty
beautiful
through
colorful
spin
toward
light
color names

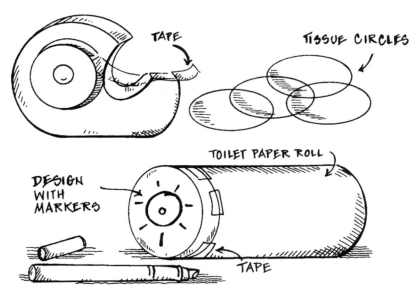

What to do

- Provide empty toilet paper rolls, tape, scissors, white tissue paper, and felt-tip markers.
- The children cut out a circle of tissue paper and draw a design with the markers.
- The children tape the circle over the end of the toilet paper roll. The kaleidoscope construction is now complete.
- The children hold the kaleidoscope to the light, look through it, rotate the tube, and describe what they see.

More

Colors can be combined in the construction phase.

Various descriptive words such as colorful and beautiful can be modeled in the actual use of the kaleidoscopes.

Questions to assess language development

EXPRESSIVE LANGUAGE

Can children use descriptors to say what they see through the kaleidoscopes?

RECEPTIVE LANGUAGE

Can children follow directions to construct the kaleidoscopes?

Literacy Connections

READING EXPERIENCES

If You Want to Find Golden by Eileen Spinelli

This book shows where many colors can be found in the city.

Mouse Paint by Ellen Stoll Walsh

Three white mice discover three jars of paint-red, blue, and yellow. When they dance and jump, they discover green, orange, and purple!

Of Colors and Things by Tana Hoban

Food, toys, and other objects are grouped together by color in this book for young children who are learning their colors.

WRITING EXPERIENCES

- Write the directions for making the kaleidoscope. Refer to the directions as you model how to make the kaleidoscope.
- Invite children to draw and write about colors in small blank books or on pieces of drawing paper.

Which Way Would You Like to Travel?

This activity gives the children an opportunity to talk about various modes of transportation as they share and chart their preferences. The finished tabulation can be posted in the room for future reference. The language emphasis here will be on social language and the ability to stay on topic for a particular category.

What you will need

Poster board

Marker for making columns

Paste or glue

Pictures of forms of transportation

Group photo of the children

Photocopies of group photo

Words you can use

transportation

airplane

chart

prefer

count

travel

bus

picture

graph

car

paste

head

number

train

What to do

- Ask the children to talk about the forms of transportation used by their families to visit relatives or take vacations. Discuss their favorite ways to travel.

- Prepare a chart with pictures from magazines that depict various forms of transportation such as a train, automobile, bus, and airplane.

- Take a group picture of the children in the class. Make a number of photocopies as this procedure can be used for other choice discussions. Cut out the outline of the children's heads from the photos.

- After the discussion of travel modes, invite each child to paste her picture in the column under the picture of her preferred form of transportation (see illustration).

- The finished chart will show the separate transportation columns. The accumulated photos of the children will indicate the mode most frequently preferred by them.

More

Follow this procedure using children's head photos for other charting activities that involve choices of preferred foods, colors, weather, and toys.

Questions to assess language development

Can children name the types of transportation being targeted?

RECEPTIVE LANGUAGE

Can they follow directions to chart their transportation preferences?

SOCIAL LANGUAGE

Can children stay on the topic through their turn and other children's turns?

Literacy Connections

READING EXPERIENCES

The Biggest Truck by David Lyon

Jim gets up when everyone else goes to sleep so he can get a load of strawberries delivered before morning.

In The Driver's Seat by Max Haynes

This very silly book puts the reader at the wheel of the car.

Tooth-Gnasher Superflash by Daniel Pinkwater

The Popsnorkle family travels in strange ways when they trade in their old Thunderclap Eight for a shiny new car that turns into things like an elephant and a flying chicken.

The Train to Gradma's by Ivan Ghantschev

Excited Marina and Jeff ride the train over bridges, through tunnels, and across a changing landscape on the way to Grandma's house.

WRITING EXPERIENCES

- Add to the finished chart by writing a sentence using each child's name and describing where she has traveled. For example, write, "Mary went to her grandma's house in a mini-van" or "Travis flew to Texas in a jet."

- Have small blank books available with titles such as "Cars," "Airplanes," and "Trains." Invite children to make their own books by drawing, writing, or dictating stories about going places using that mode of transportation.

- Turn the dramatic play area into a filling station, ticket office, or other situation. Include literacy props for children to write down orders, make tickets and receipts, create menus, etc.

Save the Earth—Recycle

This activity gives the children an opportunity to collect items that can be recycled and to communicate their findings both graphically and verbally. Matching skills and written emerging literacy will be incorporated.

What you will need

Recyclable items

Poster board

Glue or paste

Small paper tags

Marking pencil

Large drawing or painting of the earth

Words you can use

poster

recycle

save

discard

throw away

attach

find

garbage

use

save

earth

world

name

picture

What to do

- Ask the children to bring one item from home that they think can be recycled.
- Prepare a large class poster of the earth (see illustration).
- Give children paper tags to write their names on. Assist if necessary.
- Help the children attach their tags to the recycled items they brought in.
- Children glue or paste the item to a spot of their choice on the earth poster.
- The children take the class poster to other rooms and tell other children about their project.
- Hang the poster at the entrance to the center so the children can share it with parents and other visitors.

More

Children can make pictures of their houses. The children collect items from home that can be recycled and glue items to their individual pictures.

Questions to assess language development

EXPRESSIVE LANGUAGE

Can children name recyclable items?

RECEPTIVE LANGUAGE

Can children understand the concept of recycle?

Can children choose items they feel can be recycled?

Literacy Connections

READING EXPERIENCES

The Big Book for Our Planet edited by Ann Durell

> The plant Earth is honored in this wonderful collection of rhymes, tales, and essays that teach respect for our environment.

Earthdance by Joanne Ryder

> Our Earth is celebrated with beautiful language and art that will appeal to all ages of readers and listeners.

Mr. Willowby's Christmas Tree by Robert Barry

> Mr. Willowby's Christmas Tree gets recycled after the top is cut off and ultimately ends up in the home of a tiny mouse family.

WRITING EXPERIENCES

- Put recycled paper in the writing center and encourage children to write on the back.

- Help children draw, write, or dictate signs and labels encouraging others to recycle. Post them near recycling bins around the building. Be sure to use recycled paper.

Suggested Books

CIRCLE TIME

● You are Jumping

Two Is For Dancing: A One, Two, Three of Actions by Woodleigh Hubbard, Chronicle, 1991
No Jumping on the Bed by Tedd Arnold, Dial, 1997
Silly Sally by Audrey Wood, Scholastic, 1992

● Secret Message

Humbug Potion: An A-B-Cipher by Lorna Balian, Abingdon, 1984
A Kiss for Little Bear by Else H. Minarik, HarperCollins, 1968
The Secret Birthday Message by Eric Carle, Harcourt Brace, 1972

● What Do you See?

All About You by Catherine Anholt and Laurence Anholt, Viking, 1992
Brown Bear, Brown Bear, What Do You See? by Bill Martin Jr., Holt, 1996
I Went Walking by Sue Williams, Trumpet, 1989
Questions by Lee Bennet Hopkins, HarperCollins, 1992

● Stuffed Animal Mystery

Golden Bear by Ruth Young, Viking, 1992
Jamaica's Find by Juanita Havill, Houghton Mifflin, 1986
Just Look by Tana Hoban, Greenwillow, 1996
Where's My Teddy? by Jez Alborough, Candlewick, 1992

● Hot and Cold

Rebecca Rabbit Plays Hide and Seek by Evelien van Dort, Anthroposophic Press, 1997
Rosie's Walk by Pat Hutchins, Macmillan, 1968
What Game Shall We Play by Pat Hutchins, Greenwillow, 1990
Where's Spot? by Eric Hill, Putnam, 1980

● Dog Show

Bears in Pairs by Niki Yektai, Trumpet, 1987
I Love Guinea Pigs by Dick King-Smith, Candlewick, 1995
Pretend You're a Cat by Jean Marzollo, Dial, 1990

● Group Words

All About Alligators by Jim Arnosky, Scholastic, 1994
A Bundle of Beasts by Patricia Cooper, Houghton Mifflin, 1987
A Cache of Jewels by Ruth Heller, Scholastic, 1987

● I Did/What Did You Do?

Birthday Presents by Cynthia Rylant, Orchard, 1991
Friends at School by Rochelle Bunnett, Scholastic, 1995
From Head to Toe by Eric Carle, Scholastic, 1997
When I Was Little: A Four-Year-Old's Memoir of Her Youth by Jamie Lee Curtis, HarperCollins, 1993

● He or She?

Max by Rachel Isadora, Simon and Schuster, 1976
Sunshine by Jan Ormerod, Morrow, 1981
William's Doll by Charlotte Zolotow, HarperCollins, 1972

● What Does This Do?

Bigmama's by Donald Crews, Greenwillow, 1991
Eye Spy, A Mysterious Alphabet by Linda Bourke, Trumpet, 1991
The Wind Blew by Pat Hutchins, Scholastic, 1974

● How Do You Use It?

Arthur's Really Helpful Word Book by Marc Brown, Random House, 1997
Can You Guess? by Margaret Miller, Greenwillow, 1993
Is It Rough? Is It Smooth? Is It Shiny? by Tana Hoban, Greenwillow, 1984
Snowballs by Lois Ehlert, Trumpet, 1995

● Let's Sign

Communication by Aliki, Greenwillow, 1993
Handmade Alphabet by Laura Rankin, Dial, 1991
Handsigns, a Sign Language Alphabet by Kathleen Fain, Chronicle, no date

Handtalk Zoo by George Ancona and Mary B. Miller, Simon and Schuster, 1989
The Joy of Signing by Lottie L. Riekehof, Gospel Publishers, 1987

HEALTHY FOOD AND SNACKS

● Snack Time

Big Black Bear by Wong Herbert Yee, Houghton Mifflin, 1993
Pass the Fritters, Critters by Cheryl Chapman, Four Winds, 1993
Sheep Out to Eat by Nancy Shaw, Houghton Mifflin, 1992

● Setting the Table

Do Not Feed the Table by Dee Lillegard, Doubleday, 1993
How My Parents Learned to Eat by Ina R. Friedman, Houghton Mifflin, 1984

● Yummy Shapes

Bread and Jam for Frances by Russell Hoban, HarperCollins, 1960
Bread Bread Bread by Ann Morris, Lothrop, 1989

● Cooking and Learning

Benny Bakes a Cake by Eve Rice, Greenwillow, 1981
Mr. Cookie Baker by Monica Wellington, Dutton, 1992

● Yummy, Yummy

Animal Café by John Stadler, Simon and Schuster, 1980
Dinner at the Panda Palace by Stephanie Calmenson, HarperCollins, 1991
In the Diner by Christine Loomis, Scholastic, 1994

● Mystery Raisins

Eating the Alphabet: Fruits and Vegetables from A to Z by Lois Ehlert, Harcourt, 1989
Mr. Rabbit and the Lovely Present by Charlotte Zolotow, HarperCollins, 1962
What Am I? Looking Through Shapes at Apples and Grapes by N. N. Charles, Blue Sky Press, 1994

● Food Colors

Cloudy with a Chance of Meatballs by Judi Barrett, Atheneum, 1978
Growing Colors by Bruce McMillan, Lothrop, 1988
Growing Vegetable Soup by Lois Ehlert, Harcourt, 1987

● Recipes for Our Favorite Foods

Cooking Art: Easy Edible Art for Young Children by MaryAnn Kohl and Jean Potter, Gryphon House, 1997
Cup Cooking by Barbara Johnson and Betty Plemons, Early Educators Press, 1997
Fun With Kids in the Kitchen Cookbook by Judi Roger, Review and Herald, 1996
Quick and Easy Cookbook by Robyn Supraner, Troll, 1981

● The Food Pyramid

Dinosaurs Alive and Well? A Guide to Good Health by Laurence Krasny Brown and Marc Brown, Little Brown, 1990
Nutrition by Leslie Jean LeMaster, Children's Press, 1985

● Supermarket Classification

At the Supermarket by David Hautzig, Orchard, 1994
Just Shopping with Mom by Mercer Mayer, Golden, 1989
The Storekeeper by Tracey Campbell Pearson, Dial, 1985
We Keep a Store by Anne Shelby, Orchard, 1990

DRAMATIC PLAY

● A Shopping We Will Go

Feast for 10 by Cathryn Falwell, Clarion, 1993
Market! by Ted Lewin, Lothrop, 1996
Tommy at the Grocery Store by Bill Grossman, HarperCollins, 1989

● Telephone Time

Grandpa Bud by Siophan Dodds, Candlewick, 1993
Martha Speaks by Susan Meddaugh, Houghton Mifflin, 1992

● I'll Be the Mommy...

Daddies by Adele Aron Greenspan, Philomel, 1991
Octopus Hug by Laurence Pringle, Boyds Mills, 1993
This Quiet Lady by Charlotte Zolotow, Greenwillow, 1992
What Will Mommy Do When I'm at School? by Dolores Johnson, Macmillan, 1990

● Clothes Have Names Too

Aaron's Shirt by Deborah Gould, Bradbury, 1989
The Dress I'll Wear to the Party by Shirley Neitzel, Greenwillow, 1992
Froggy Gets Dressed by Jonathan London, Viking, 1992
Mary Wore Her Red Dress and Henry Wore His Green Sneakers by Merle Peek, Clarion, 1985

● Wash Day

Froggy Gets Dressed by Jonathan London, Viking, 1992
Mrs. McNosh Hangs Up Her Wash by Sarah Weeks, HarperCollins, 1998

● Hats

Caps for Sale by Esphyr Slobodkina, HarperCollins, 1947
The Night Ones by Patricia Grossman, Harcourt Brace, 1991
Whose Hat? by Margaret Miller, Greenwillow, 1988

● First Aid Station

The Bear's Toothache by David McPhail, Little Brown, 1972
The Checkup by Helen Oxenbury, Puffin, 1994
My Doctor by Harlow Rockwell, Macmillan, 1992
My First Doctor Visit by Julia Allen, ARO Publishing, 1987

● Pet Shop

Herbie Hamster, Where Are You? by Terence Blacker, Random House, 1990
I Really Want a Dog by S. Blakemore and S. Breslow, Puffin, 1993
Michael and the Cats by Barbara Abercrombie, Simon and Schuster, 1993
No Plain Pets! by Marc Barasch, HarperCollins, 1991
Scruffy by Peggy Parish, HarperCollins, 1988

● Beach Party

A Beach Day by Douglas Florian, Greenwillow, 1990
Harry by the Sea by Gene Zion, HarperCollins, 1965
Just Grandma and Me by Mercer Mayer, Golden, 1985

● Shadow Creatures

Bear Shadow by Frank Asch, Simon & Schuster, 1988
Hanimations by Mario Mariotti, Kane/Miller, 1989
Henry and the Dragon by Eileen Christelow, Clarion, 1984
I Have a Friend by Keiko Narahashi, Simon and Schuster, 1987
It Looked Like Spilt Milk by Charles G. Shaw, HarperCollins, 1947

● Mommy and Daddy Helpers

Daddy Makes the Best Spaghetti by Anna Grossnickle Hines, Houghton Mifflin, 1986
Farm Morning by David McPhail, Harcourt Brace, 1991
Pig Pig Gets a Job by David McPhail, Dutton, 1990

● Where Do I Belong?

The Old Woman Who Named Things by Cynthia Rylant, Harcourt Brace, 1996
Pots and Pans by Anne Rockwell, Macmillan, 1993
Where Does It Go? by Margaret Miller, Greenwillow, 1992

● What Does My Face Say?

I Like It When by Mary Murphy, Harcourt Brace, 1997
I Was So Mad by Norma Simon, Whitman, 1974
The Temper Tantrum Book by Edna Preston Mitchell, Puffin, 1976

● Where Do I Live?

Is Your Mama a Llama? by Deborah Guarino, Scholastic, 1989
A Nice Walk in the Jungle by Nan Bodsworth, Dutton, 1992
One Red Rooster by Kathleen Sullivan Carroll, Houghton Mifflin, 1992

● "What Am I?"

All the Way Home by Lore Segal, Farrar, 1973
Good-Night, Owl! by Pat Hutchins, Macmillan, 1972
Let's Go Home, Little Bear by Martin Waddell, Candlewick, 1993

● I Am.....

At the Laundromat by Christine Loomis, Scholastic, 1993
Just for You by Mercer Mayer, Golden, 1975
What's What? A Guessing Game by Mary Serfozo, Simon and Schuster, 1996

OUTDOOR PLAY

● Parachutes

First Flight by David McPhail, Little Brown, 1991
Into This Night We Are Rising by Jonathon London, Viking, 1993
Rainy Day Dream by Michael Chesworth, Farrar, 1992
Tomorrow, Up and Away! by Pat L. Collins, Houghton Mifflin, 1990
The Wing Shop by Elvira Woodruff, Holiday, 1991

● I Love a Parade

The Jacket I Wear in the Snow by Shirley Neitzel, Greenwillow, 1989
Shoes From Grandpa by Mem Fox, Orchard, 1990
There's a Party at Mona's Tonight by Harry Allard, Doubleday, 1981

● Listening Parade

Listen to the Rain by Bill Martin, Jr. and John Archambault, Henry Holt, 1988
The Listening Walk by Paul Showers, HarperCollins, 1991
What Noise? by Debbie MacKinnon, Dial, 1993
Zin! Zin! Zin!: A Violin by Lloyd Moss, Simon and Schuster, 1995

● Teddy Bear Picnic

Picnic by Emily A. McCully, HarperCollins, 1984
It's the Bear by Jez Alborough, Candlewick Press, 1994

The Rattlebang Picnic by Margaret Mahy, Dial Books, 1994

● Egg Hunt

The Best Easter Egg Hunt Ever by John Speirs, Scholastic, 1997
Easter Egg Artists by Adrienne Adams, Simon and Schuster, 1991
The Easter Egg Farm by Mary Jane Auch, Holiday House, 1992

● Going Fishing

Fishing by Diana Engle, Macmillan, 1993
Fishing Sunday by Tony Johnston, Morrow, 1996
Fishing with Dad by Michael J. Rosen, Artisan, 1996
McElligot's Pool by Dr. Seuss, Random House, 1947

● Let's Paint

Mouse Paint by Ellen Walsh, Harcourt Brace, 1989
Oh, Were They Ever Happy! by Peter Spier, Doubleday, 1978
Over-Under by Catherine Matthias, Children's Press, 1984

● Stop and Go

Barn Dance! by Bill Martin, Jr. and John Archambault, Henry Holt, 1986
Dance Away by George Shannon, Greenwillow, 1982
Hop Jump by Ellen Stoll Walsh, Harcourt, 1993
Max by Rachel Isodora, Macmillan, 1976

● Red Light, Green Light

The Farmer in the Dell by Ilse Plume, Hyperion, 1988
Jeremy's Tail by Duncan Ball, Orchard, 1991
Playing Sardines by Beverly Major, Scholastic, 1988

● Falling Leaves Tree Match

Red Leaf, Yellow Leaf by Lois Ehlert, Harcourt Brace, 1991
Why Do Leaves Change Color? by Betsy Maestro, HarperCollins, 1994

Adventure Walk

Nature Walk by Douglas Florian, Greenwillow, 1989

The Perfect Spot by Robert J. Blake, Philomel, 1992

What Joe Saw by Anna Grossnickle Hines, Greenwillow, 1994

ART

Tell Me About Your Picture

Cool Ali by Nancy Poydar, McElderry Books, 1996

Emma's Rug by Allen Say, Houghton Mifflin, 1996

The Fantastic Drawings of Danielle by Barbara McClintock, Houghton Mifflin, 1996

Art Show

Art Dog by Thacher Hurd, HarperCollins, 1996

The Paper Princess by Elisa Kleven, Dutton, 1994

Regina's Big Mistake by Marissa Moss, Houghton Mifflin, 1990

Color Creations

Color by Ruth Heller, Putnam, 1995

Little Blue and Little Yellow by Leo Lionni, Scholastic, 1993

Mouse Paint by Ellen Stoll Walsh, Scholastic, 1989

White Rabbit's Color Book by Alan Baker, Scholastic 1994

All Bark No Bites

A B Cedar: An Alphabet of Trees by George Ella Lyon, Orchard, 1989

A Tree Is Nice by Janice May Udry, HarperCollins, 1981

Have You Seen Trees? by Joanne Oppenheim, Scholastic, 1995

Red Leaf, Yellow Leaf by Lois Ehlert, Harcout Brace, 1991

Color Rubbings

The Color Box by Dayle Ann Dodds, Little Brown, 1992

Color Dance by Ann Jonas, Greenwillow, 1989

Lunch by Denise Fleming, Henry Holt, 1992

Make a Shape

Grandfather Tang's Story by Ann Tompert, Crown, 1990

Sea Shapes by Suse MacDonald, Harcourt, 1994

The Secret Birthday Message by Eric Carle, HarperCollins, 1972

Sound Pictures

Early Morning in the Barn by Nancy Tafuri, Greenwillow, 1983

Pots and Pans by Patricia Hubbell, HarperCollins, 1998

Splash, Splash by Jeff Sheppard, Simon and Schuster, 1994

The Wheels Go Around

How Many Trucks Can a Tow Truck Tow? by Charlotte Pomerantz, Random House, 1987

My Bike by Donna Jakob, Hyperion, 1994

Train Song by Diane Siebert, HarperCollins, 1990

Places We Go

Emma's Vacation by David McPhail, Dutton, 1987

The Journey Home by Alison Lester, Houghton Mifflin, 1991

Love, Your Bear Pete by Dyan Sheldon, Candlewick, 1994

How Did You Go?

Dinosaurs Travel by Laura K. Brown and Marc Brown, Little Brown, 1991

This is the Way We Go to School: A Book About Children Around the World by Edith Baer, Scholastic, 1990

The Wheels on the Bus by Maryann Kovalski, Little Brown, 1987

Snowman

Snow Magic by Harriet Ziefert, Viking, 1988

Snowballs by Lois Ehlert, Trumpet, 1995

Snowy Day by Ezra Jack Keats, Puffin, 1976

Winter Play

Ice Cream Bear by Jez Alborough, Scholastic, 1989

It's Snowing! It's Snowing! by Jack Prelutsky, Greenwillow, 1984

Katy and the Big Snow by Virginia Lee Burton, Houghton Mifflin, 1973

Snow on Snow on Snow by Cheryl Chapman, Dial, 1994

- Topic Collages

My First Riddles by Judith Hoffman Corwin, HarperCollins, 1998

The Paper Dragon by Marguerite W. Davol, Simon and Schuster, 1997

Rooster's Off to See the World by Eric Carle, Simon and Schuster, 1991

- Popsicle Puppets

Onstage and Backstage at the Night Owl Theatre by Ann Hayes, Harcourt Brace, 1997

The Three Billy Goats Gruff illustrated by Stephen Carpenter, HarperCollins, 1998

- Emotion Puppets

Feelings by Aliki, Greenwillow Books, 1984

How Do I Feel? by Norma Simon, Albert Whitman, 1970

Mean Soup by Betsy Everitt, Harcourt, 1992

My Many Colored Days by Dr. Seuss, Knopf, 1996

- A Special Card for You

Birthdays! Celebrating Life Around the World by Eve B. Feldman, Bridge Water Books, 1996

Don't Forget to Write by Marina Selway, Ideals Children's Books, 1994

SAND AND WATER

- Color Fish

A Color of His Own by Leo Lionni, Alfred A. Knopf, 1975

Fish Is Fish by Leo Lionni, Alfred A. Knopf, 1970

The Rainbow Fish by Marcus Pfister, North-South Books, 1992

- Bubble Talk

Bubble Bubble by Mercer Mayer, Troll, 1973

- Wash the Dishes

Feast for Ten by Cathryn Falwell, Houghton Mifflin, 1993

- Highway in the Sand

The Biggest Truck by David Lyon, Lothrop, 1988

Night Ride by Bernie Karlin and Mati Karlin, Simon and Schuster, 1988

Truck Song by Diane Siebert, Crowell, 1984

- Sand Table Landscaping

Building a House by Byron Barton, Greenwillow, 1981

Castle Builder by Dennis Nolan, Macmillan, no date

The Little House by Virginia Lee Burton, Houghton Mifflin, 1978

This Is My House by Arthur Dorros, Scholastic, 1992

- Water Drop Magnifier

A Drop of Water by Walter Wick, Scholastic, 1997

- Water Feelings and Looks

My Life With the Wave by Catherine Cowan, Lothrop, 1997

Until I Saw the Sea: A Collection of Seashore Poems, edited by Alison Shaw, Holt, 1995

- Look What I Found

Do You See a Mouse? by Bernard Waber, Houghton Mifflin, 1995

Don't Tell the Whole World! by Joanna Cole, Crowell, 1990

Nanta's Lion: A Search-and-Find Adventure by Audrey Wood, Morrow, 1995

- Measuring

Inch by Inch by Leo Lionni, Astor-Honor, 1960

The Line-up Book by Marisabina Russo, Greenwillow, 1986

- Opposites

Big and Little by Steve Jenkins, Houghton Mifflin, 1996

Demi's Opposites: An Animal Game Book by Demi, Grosset and Dunlap, 1987

Exactly the Opposite by Tana Hoban, Greenwillow Books, 1990

What the Moon Saw by Brian Wildsmith, Oxford University Press, 1978

MUSIC AND MOVEMENT

● Kitchen Band

All Join In by Quentin Blake, Little Brown, 1991

Mama Don't Allow by Thacher Hurd, HarperCollins, 1984

Thump, Thump, Tat-a-Tat-Tat by Gene Baer, HarperCollins, 1991

● Junky Funky Music

Crash! Bang! Boom! by Peter Spier, Doubleday, 1990

The Happy Hedgehog Band by Martin Waddell, Candlewick, 1992

● Move and Groove

Fiddle-I-Fee: A Farmyard Song for the Very Young by Melissa Sweet, Little Brown, 1994

I Know an Old Lady Who Swallowed a Fly by Glen Rounds, Holiday, 1990

This Old Man by Carol Jones, Houghton Mifflin, 1990

The Three Little Kittens by Lorinda Bryan Cauley, Putnam, 1984

● Weather Moves

Did You Hear Wind Sing Your Name? by Sandra De Coteau Orie, Walker, 1995

Rain Talk by Mary Serfozo, Simon and Schuster, 1990

Windsongs and Rainbows by Albert Burton, Simon and Schuster, 1993

● Monkey in the Middle

Caps for Sale by Esphyr Slobodkina, Scholastic, 1993

Five Little Monkeys Sitting in a Tree by Eileen Christoleow, Houghton Mifflin, 1991

Monkey See, Monkey Do by Marc Gave, Scholastic, 1993

● Follow Me

Make Way for Ducklings by Robert McClosky, Puffin, 1976

Too Much by Dorothy Stott, Dutton, no date

Up the Wall by Nicholas Heller, Greenwillow, 1992

● Backwards Fun

Silly Sally by Audrey Wood, Harcourt Brace, 1992

● Dance Party

Barn Dance! by Bill Martin Jr. and John Archambault, Henry Holt, 1986

Color Dance by Ann Jonas, Greenwillow, 1989

The Moon Jumpers by Janice May Udry, HarperCollins, 1959

● Quiet Time

Going to Sleep on the Farm by Wendy Cheyette Lewison, Dial, 1992

The Napping House by Audrey Wood, Harcourt Brace, 1984

Naptime, Laptime by Eileen Spinelli, Scholastic, 1995

Sleep Tight by B.G. Hennessy, Viking, 1992

● Let's Make Some Noise

At Mary Bloom's by Aliki, Greenwillow, 1983

Meet the Marching Smithereens by Ann Hayes, Harcourt Brace, 1995

Poems Go Clang: A Collection of Noisey Verse by Debi Gliori, Candlewick, 1997

Polar Bear, Polar Bear, What Do You Hear? by Bill Martin Jr., Henry Holt, 1991

● Quick as a Cricket

Five Minutes Peace by Jill Murphy, Talman, no date

My Many Colored Days by Dr. Seuss, Random House, 1996

The Very Quiet Cricket by Eric Carle, Putnam, 1997

● Where Would You Hide If You Were The Gingerbread Man?

The Gingerbread Boy by Richard Egielski, HarperCollins, 1997

You Can't Catch Me by Charlotte Doyle, HarperCollins, 1997

● Singing Helpers

The Farmer in the Dell by Ilse Plume, Hyperion, 1995

Take Me Out to the Ballgame by Jack Norworth, Simon and Schuster, 1992

Today is Monday by Eric Carle, Putnam, 1993

The Wheels on the Bus by Maryann Kovalski, Little Brown, 1990

MATH

- Shape Bingo

Grandfather Tang's Story by Ann Tompert

A Pair of Socks by Stuart J. Murphy, HarperCollins, 1997

- Fruit Pieces

Eating Fractions by Bruce McMillan, Scholastic, 1991

Eating the Alphabet: Fruits and Vegetables From A to Z by Lois Ehlert, Harcourt Brace, 1989

Give Me Half by Stuart J. Murphy, HarperCollins, 1997

- What's Missing

Five Little Ducks by Rafi, Crown, 1988

Moon Jump: A Countdown by Paula Brown, Viking, 1992

- Shop 'til You Drop

Pigs Will Be Pigs by Amy Axelrod, Four Winds, 1994

Sheep in a Shop by Nancy Shaw, Houghton Mifflin, 1991

A Chair for My Mother by Vera Williams, Greenwillow, 1982

Uno, Dos, Tres: 1,2,3 by Pat Mora, Houghton Mifflin, 1996

- So Big

The Story of Imelda, Who Was Small by Lurie Morris, Houghton Mifflin, 1988

The Best Bug Parade by Stuart Murphy, HarperCollins, 1997

Inch by Inch by Leo Lionni, Astor-Honor, 1960

- Higher and Higher

George Shrinks by William Joyce, HarperCollins, 1985

Just a Little Bit by Ann Tompert, Houghton Mifflin, 1993

The Line-up Book by Marisabina Russo, Greenwillow, 1986

Tiny for a Day by Dick Gackenbach, Clarion, 1993

- Cubby Counting

One, Two, One Pair! by Bruce McMillan, Scholastic, 1991

Ten Cats Have Hats: A Counting Book by Jean Marzollo, Scholastic, 1994

This Old Man by Carol Jones, Houghton Mifflin, 1990

- Counting My Toes

Let's Count It Out, Jesse Bear by Nancy White Carlstrom, Simon and Schuster, 1996

- Number Hunt

How Many, How Many, How Many by Rick Walton, Candlewick, 1993

Ten Black Dots by Donald Crews, Greenwillow, 1986

More Than One by Miriam Schlein, Greenwillow, 1996

- The M & M Challenge

Every Buddy Counts by Stuart J. Murphy, HarperCollins, 1997

Hippos Go Berserk by Sandra Boynton, Simon and Schuster, 1996

The M & M's Brand Chocolate Candies Counting Book by Barbara McGrath, Charlesbridge, 1994

- Number People

Count! by Denise Fleming, Henry Holt, 1992

Big Fat Hen by Keith Baker, Harcourt Brace, 1994

One Red Rooster by Kathleen Sullivan Carroll, Houghton Mifflin, 1992

What Comes in Twos, Threes and Fours? by Suzanne Aker, Simon and Schuster, 1990

SCIENCE

- Animal Homes

Any Room for Me? by Loek Koopmans, Floris, no date

A House is a House for Me by Mary Ann Hoberman, Viking, 1978

Is This a House for Hermit Crab? by Megan McDonald, Orchard, 1990

Where do Bears Sleep? by Barbara Shook Hazen, HarperCollins, 1997

● Behind the Wall

Mac and Marie and the Train Toss Surprise by Elizabeth Howard, Simon and Schuster, 1993
Once There was a Bull...(Frog) by Rick Walton, Gibbs Smith, 1995
Peck, Slither, and Slide by Suse MacDonald, Harcourt Brace, 1997
What Am I? Looking Through Shapes at Apples and Grapes by N.N. Charles, Scholastic, 1994

● Touch and Tell

I Can Tell By Touching by Carolyn Otto, HarperCollins, 1994
Night Sounds, Morning Colors by Rosemary Wells, Dial, 1994
Sense Suspense: A Guessing Game for the Five Senses by Bruce McMillan, Scholastic, 1994

● How Does It Feel

Fuzzy Yellow Ducklings by Matthew Van Fleet, Dial, 1995
The Very Busy Spider by Eric Carl, Putnam, 1985
Windsongs and Rainbows by Albert Burton, Simon and Schuster, 1993

● Weight Time

Everybody Needs a Rock by Byrd Baylor, Simon and Schuster, 1974
The Mouse and the Potato by Thomas Berger and Carla Grillis, Gryphon House, 1990

● The Big Stick-Up

Harvey Potter's Balloon Farm by Jerdine Nolen, Lothrop, 1994
The Way Things Work by David Macaulay, Houghton Mifflin, 1988

● Space Mud

Bartholomew and the Oobleck by Dr. Seuss, Random House, 1949
Clay Boy by Mirra Ginsberg, Putnam, 1993
Mud Pies and Other Recipes: A Cookbook for Dolls by Marjorie Winslow, Walker, 1996

● Pollution Solution

Dinosaurs to the Rescue! A Guide to Protecting Our Planet by Laurene Krasny Brown and Marc Brown, Little Brown, 1992
Prince William by Gloria Rand, Henry Holt, 1992
Someday a Tree by Eve Bunting, Houghton Mifflin, 1993

● Kaleidoscope

If You Want to Find Golden by Eileen Spinelli, Whitman, 1993
Mouse Paint by Ellen Stoll Walsh, Harcourt Brace, 1989
Of Colors and Things by Tana Hoban, Greenwillow, 1989

● Which Way Would You Like to Travel

The Biggest Truck by David Lyon, Lothrop, 1988
In The Driver's Seat by Max Haynes, Doubleday, 1997
Tooth-Gnasher Superflash by Daniel Pinkwater, Simon and Schuster, 1990
The Train to Grandma's by Ivan Ghantschev, Simon and Schuster, no date

● Save The Earth—Recycle

The Big Book for Our Planet edited by Ann Durell, Dutton, no date
Earthdance by Joanne Ryder, Henry Holt, 1996
Mr. Willowby's Christmas Tree by Robert Barry, Buccaneer, 1992

Index